I0118090

And I Cried, Too

Confronting Evil in a Small Town

—a memoir—

Mike Hartnett

A MEADOWLARK BOOK

Meadowlark (an imprint of Chasing Tigers Press)
meadowlark-books.com
PO Box 333, Emporia, KS 66801

Copyright © 2019 Mike Hartnett

Author photo by Michelle Kelly

All rights reserved.

This book and parts thereof may not be reproduced in any form, stored in a retrieval system, or transmitted in any forms by any means—electronic, mechanical, photocopy, recording, or otherwise—without prior written permission of the publisher, except as provided by United States of America copyright law.

This book is a work of non-fiction; conversations and details are taken from the author's memories and from the author's perspective. Some names have been fictionalized, as the author felt appropriate.

ISBN: 978-1-7322410-8-4

Library of Congress Control Number: 2019949853

Dedication

To my wife of fifty-one years, Barbara, the North Star of my life, who lived with me and supported me through what's recounted here.

To the late William Maxwell, the noted novelist and former editor of *The New Yorker*, without whose support and direction I never would have written this book.

To Brian Daldorph, without whose support I never would have finished this book.

To Mitch Favus, who gave me Mr. Maxwell's book, *So Long, See You Tomorrow*, which started the process.

To the men in the writing group at the Douglas County (KS) jail, who nagged me to finish the book.

Chapters

As Dickens said,
"It was the best of times,
it was the worst of times."
The years in Lincoln, Illinois, were both.
Great friends, great students, great life.
Then the murders started.

*A Tale of Two Cities

Chapter I

This is how I remember my years at Lincoln College. There may be a few places where I inadvertently stray from exactly what happened, but looking back, that's not so important; this is my memory.

I could have returned to Lincoln, Illinois, and interviewed the victims, the relatives, the college personnel, and the police. I could have asked them to tear open whatever emotional bandages time has given them. Then I would have been certain of every detail, but the cost would be too high. Anyway, it's the memories and the scars that live on.

Except for Mike Mansfield and Russ Smrekar, I have changed the names of the students. They've had enough.

To all those involved, let me quote the late William Maxwell's wish in his novel, *So Long, See You Tomorrow*:

> "… whether all that finally began to seem less real, more like something they dreamed, so that instead of being stuck there, they could go on and by the grace of God lead their own lives, undestroyed by what was not their doing."

● ● ●

The best way to summarize the Lincoln, Illinois, we discovered in 1972 is to talk about Gem Lunch, a modest little restaurant run by a second-generation Greek immigrant, Pete Andrews. The Gem was a gathering place where jovial, busy waitresses walked down narrow aisles to serve enormous meals to Pete's friends.

Pete cooked as if his food could cure heartache. His basic breakfast—for about two and a half dollars—was two eggs, numerous strips of bacon, hash browns, one pancake, a pineapple slice, and a red grape. Often he would look from the kitchen to see who had placed the order. If it was a friend, he'd cook a third egg.

The luncheon specials always included great mashed potatoes and gravy with every main course, whether it was roast beef, roast pork, chop suey, or spaghetti.

Pete cooked for everyone, including those who couldn't pay, and served many a free meal during the Depression. The Gem was the first restaurant in town to serve African Americans, long before most white Americans ever thought about desegregation.

Seventeen thousand people lived in Lincoln, which was founded more than 150 years earlier in the middle of some of the richest farmland in the world.

Lincoln was just far enough away from bigger towns that it developed its own friendly character; it wasn't a suburb. No matter where they worked—thirty miles away in Bloomington, Springfield, or Decatur, or sixty miles away in Champaign or Peoria—residents felt living in Lincoln was worth the drive.

Why?

Because small-town stereotypes were true.

There was perhaps a murder once every half decade, so most people never thought to lock their doors. The newspaper published stinging editorials on the burning of leaves, and the high school basketball coach had his own show on the local radio station. Mama Sorrento at Sorrento's Pizzeria always put free anchovies on my pizza because, she claimed, she and I were the only ones in town who liked them.

People drove like they'd reach their local destination in five minutes, and they would, too.

As some townsfolk described it a while back, a slick Springfield lawyer named Abe Lincoln helped pull a fast one on the folks at neighboring Mt. Pulaski and had the county seat moved to Lincoln. "And don't think those folks have forgotten it, either," they'd add with a smile.

If a neighbor became sick in Lincoln, folks would drop in with enough food to last until the illness was just a memory. Folks didn't *talk* to each other; however, they would *visit* with each other.

Lincoln was a revelation to my wife Barbara and me, both twenty-six when we arrived in June of 1972. Raised in Chicago and educated at the sprawling University of Illinois, we were unaccustomed to the subtle pleasures of small-town living. We eventually bought a home that had once belonged to a long-deceased political leader. When we needed a washing machine delivered to the house from the local Sears store, we gave the salesman our address: 104 N. Union.

"Where's that," he asked.

"Well, it's just a few blocks away, at the corner of Union and Eighth." I thought it strange that he would have to ask.

"Oh, you mean the old Madigan house," he said with a smile.

From then on, we never gave townspeople our address. We'd just say, "the old Madigan house," and everyone knew.

Perhaps if we had grown up in Lincoln, we wouldn't have appreciated it as much. We would have taken for granted the wonderful old homes, the evening walks down the tree-lined streets, the relaxed pace, and the peace.

Besides the county fair and the rail-splitting festival with its cow-chip-throwing event, there wasn't much night life. That was all right. We had more pleasure gathering with good friends for dinner than we ever did in a Chicago night club. And it was so easy to make good friends in Lincoln.

We did wonder, though, how long it would take before our home became "the old Hartnett house."

• • •

At the northeast edge of Lincoln sat the reason we came to town: Lincoln College—a small, private junior college founded as a Presbyterian school for ministerial students shortly after the Civil War. The only college named for Abraham Lincoln before his assassination, the college had dropped its religious affiliation and become a two-year school in the 1940s. Five dorms housed about four-hundred students who attended classes with about one-hundred or so townsfolk. The curriculum was liberal arts, and most students enrolled with the goal of eventually transferring to a four-year college.

If Gem Lunch epitomized the best of the town, then the college's "Prayer Meetings" personified the best of the small college. Most Friday afternoons after four, anyone from the college who was thirsty for beer or conversation would drop into a local bar named Bachelors III. (This was when the drinking age had been lowered to nineteen, and before it was raised again.)

A typical Friday afternoon would see a dorm director sitting with three of his residents berating the Chicago

Bears, a faculty member telling students about his alma mater, Barbara explaining to a would-be psychology major what can and can't be done with a psych degree, the student senate president pressing a dean for changes in quiet hours rules in the dorms, and a basketball player telling me he should be in the starting lineup. It was a far cry from our experience at the huge University of Illinois campus.

If a particular "Prayer Meeting" lasted beyond the closing of the nearby college dining hall, Barbara and I would often invite whoever was left to the old Madigan house for hamburgers. The students who came to our home were the typical Lincoln College stereotype— frightened teenagers who enrolled because other schools wouldn't accept them. They attended class for two years, matured, earned better grades than ever before, and transferred to four-year colleges.

The problems they caused, and had, were minor. They used the college as it was intended to be used, and they moved on.

Many of the white students seemed to be the runt of the litter. Did they all have older brothers and sisters who were brilliant doctors or lawyers, or did it just seem that way?

Many of the African American students, away from city ghettos and living near cornfields for the first time, suffered from culture shock.

Lincoln wasn't what we expected, but after we overcame our own culture shock, Barbara and I found it was easy to like these kids.

Sometimes, though, we thought the school was too small, too informal. Most graduates would transfer to a large state university (after two years at Lincoln, some couldn't afford a private school anymore) and some had trouble adjusting to large lecture classes, huge dormitories, and using their ID numbers instead of names.

Lincoln's teachers were almost too good. Some students would become so excited about a field that they'd decide to major in it. A couple of years later, after being taught by university professors who weren't so caring, so personal, so charismatic, they'd conclude that earth science wasn't so interesting after all.

Barbara and I arrived, fresh with our master's degrees. I was hired as the college's only full-time counselor, and Barbara was a counselor and dormitory director.

We were nervous at first, remembering the full staff of Ph.D.'s and psychiatrists in the campus counseling center at the University of Illinois. But looking at the peaceful little campus before the students arrived, we wondered, "How serious could any student's problems be in a school like this? In a town like this?"

We soon learned the answer.

Chapter II

It was the students, of course, who were the heart of the college. Most of them, we loved. Some broke our hearts. A few, we wanted expelled. A handful made us feel frustrated because we didn't have the training or expertise to give them the help they needed. What follows is a sample of the various students who became a part of our lives.

• • •

One delightful student, Steve, had a severe case of cerebral palsy; it was painful to watch him walk. After a nasty ice storm hit Lincoln, most of the students stayed in their dorm rooms, but not Steve. He wasn't going to let a damn ice storm stop him from going to class. He began walking, and sure enough, he fell and lay on his back for a moment.

Rosemary, perhaps the prettiest and nicest girl on campus, saw Steve and waddled across the ice, bent over, and said, "Steve! Can I do anything for you?"

Steve looked up at this beautiful young woman, sighed, and answered, "How 'bout a little mouth-to-mouth resuscitation?"

• • •

Darwin, a freshman art major from a Chicago, was attending Lincoln on a wrestling scholarship. He was married, and Lincoln didn't have facilities for married students, so I helped him find an apartment near campus through the local public housing office.

I didn't realize what type of person Darwin was until the next day when he sat in my waiting room for forty-five minutes just to say thanks for helping him find the apartment.

He and his wife Juanetta were quiet, handsome people and obviously deeply in love.

They were also desperately poor; their living room had nothing but a single chair bought at a used furniture store. I never saw Darwin wear anything except a white T-shirt and blue jeans. That, of course, was the uniform of college students in the mid-70s, but the difference for Darwin, which I realized when he politely declined to attend a dinner at the house of the college's president, was that he had nothing else to wear.

For two months Juanetta waitressed at the counter of the local Woolworth's while Darwin attended classes and practiced with the wrestling team. I saw them occasionally at campus activities—always close together and smiling.

One day Darwin burst into my office with a wide, gleaming smile: Juanetta was pregnant.

Darwin was quietly aglow for two months until Juanetta had to quit her job because of problems with the pregnancy.

Three months later, while Darwin was wrestling in a tournament in Chicago, a neighbor found Juanetta unconscious on the living room floor. She was rushed to the hospital in labor.

We contacted the wrestling coach who immediately drove Darwin to the hospital. I spent the night in the emergency waiting room with him as he alternated between quiet tears and shocked silence.

The baby died about 3:00 AM. Juanetta was kept alive through life support systems. The doctor said the cause was toxic eclampsia, or some such thing. He said if he worked for a year in a big city public hospital, he probably would not see such a severe case.

Darwin refused to leave the hospital while Juanetta clung to life. After forty-eight hours, I returned home without him. Juanetta remained in a coma. Darwin just sat in the waiting room.

While sitting there one night, Darwin met a woman whose son had left some painting supplies at home when he joined the Army. When Darwin told her he was an art major, she brought the supplies to him the next day. He thanked the woman and began painting in the waiting room

Students would bring him clothes, and I periodically tried to convince him to return home for some rest. His mother rode the train from Chicago to talk to him, but he would not leave Juanetta. He just kept waiting—and painting.

The days stretched into weeks, and the weeks turned into a month. Darwin kept painting.

Hospital staff members noticed his work and offered him money for his paintings. I don't know if the doctors and nurses bought them out of pity or appreciation of his talent. I do know he made enough money to buy all of his meals in the hospital cafeteria.

One night Juanetta's body had had enough, and she died quietly. Darwin gathered up his art supplies and finally went home.

The hospital bill was more than $250,000. It might as well have been $25 million.

I drove some of Darwin's classmates to Chicago for the funeral and was shocked by Darwin's appearance—a hollow shell of the smiling young wrestler-artist I had known.

After the burial he told me he was going to drop out of school. He had missed so many classes, he said, and anyway, he didn't see much point in school anymore.

Darwin stayed in Chicago after the funeral. I thought about him often, and three years later, when I was writing for a newspaper, I called his mother trying to find him. She said he was working part-time as a security guard, still trying to pay off the hospital bill. She said he was just about the same as I had seen him at the funeral.

She added, "They were just two good, kind kids trying to get ahead."

• • •

John was a six-foot, three-inch, 220-pound lump of malevolence, nicknamed Mad Dog by students who seemed too frightened to explain why. Mad Dog was unconcerned with studying, the college's rules, or other students. He did what he wanted, regardless of the consequences.

This was tough on the dorm directors because, for students like Mad Dog, there were no consequences. We quickly learned that the college had serious financial problems, so expulsion was almost never an option. Every time a dorm director would report Mad Dog, Lincoln's new dean of students would give the student a lecture. Mad Dog would just glare at him and not change his behavior.

He was caught raising hell in the dorms—again—blaring his stereo at 3:00 AM. The students on the floor couldn't sleep but were afraid to ask him to turn down the volume. The music blared until the dorm director heard it two floors away.

When Mad Dog received only another lecture, I went over the dean's head to the president and asked how we were supposed to keep the lid on and help the other students with Mad Dog around.

"Tell you what," he responded. "How about if I call him into my office and ask for his cooperation?"

As we spoke, Barbara caught Mad Dog ripping a water fountain off its floor support in her dorm. Finally, *finally*, he was expelled.

He was the extreme exception. There were a few (very few, thank god) other cases like Mad Dog, all usually handled the same way.

● ● ●

One of the residents in Barbara's dorms, Cheryl, came to Lincoln from Louisville. She was a nice, lonely kid who meant well the few hours a day she wasn't high.

Attending class was often out of the question for her. We tried to help, but she was so numb from pills most of the time that I don't think she understood what we said.

Barbara and I pleaded with the dean to do something, anything, before Cheryl overdosed. We kept nagging him like shrewish wives with no success until finally Barbara received a phone call from the Illinois Bureau of Investigation asking her to meet with an officer in the back room of a local drug store.

Apparently the pharmacist became suspicious when Cheryl repeatedly asked for refills on her drugs because she had "lost" them. He alerted the IBI. During the investigation, the IBI got the license plate number of a good student who had simply given Cheryl a ride to the drug store.

The IBI agent wanted to know if Cheryl's chauffer was part of a drug ring.

That was the last straw. Now innocent kids were being dragged into Cheryl's problem. Finally the dean agreed to call Cheryl's mother in Louisville. He told her the entire story: Barbara was afraid she'd find Cheryl dead from an overdose one day.

They both told the mother that Cheryl needed to be put in a drug rehab program back in Kentucky. The mother responded, "Why Kentucky? Isn't there a rehab program in Illinois you could send her to?"

The dean shouted, "She's YOUR daughter!"

"Oh, okay," the mother said.

Cheryl and Mad Dog left us, but not without exacting a price. We were relieved they were gone and now someone else's responsibility, but that relief was coupled with feelings of anger, failure, inadequacy, and guilt. And with each case, we learned a little about ourselves.

• • •

During one Parents' Weekend, a couple came to me and, with tears in their eyes, thanked me for all the college had done for their son, Fred. His mother called us "miracle workers."

I accepted their gratitude because they needed to thank someone, but I knew we weren't miracle workers. Apparently Fred had raised hell in grade school and early high school; school officials considered him a juvenile delinquent and treated him as such.

Fred acted accordingly.

We didn't know he was a delinquent; we thought he was just another nice, normal kid, and we treated him that way.

Fred acted accordingly.

All we had done was accept a nice young kid who had been lost in his high school and given him a positive change of scenery and a little support—and how much more support could we have given him if we hadn't been so preoccupied with the Cheryls and the Mad Dogs.

• • •

Martha was from a country in Africa—I don't remember which one. All of the arrangements (enrollment, assignment to an advisor, housing) were made by mail. Shortly before the fall semester was to begin, her advisor received a telegram saying she would be flying into Lincoln on a major airline.

There was an issue, however. Lincoln didn't have an airport capable of accommodating a large commercial airplane. Frantic phone calls followed, and we learned that she was flying to Lincoln, Nebraska, not Lincoln, Illinois.

Apparently Martha had asked for a ticket to "Lincoln in America," not knowing there was more than one Lincoln. Could be the travel agent didn't know either, so when he looked on a map and saw Lincoln, he figured that's where she wanted to go.

By the time we realized all this, Martha was on her flight. Fortunately, a faculty member had a pilot's license and was always happy for a reason to fly. He and Martha's advisor rented a plane and flew to Nebraska, just in time to greet Martha at the airport and inform her that she had one more flight to take. Talk about personal attention.

Once she was settled in the right Lincoln, Martha was a fascinating delight. No taller than five feet, her skin was as black as coal. She had a cherubic face, and a British accent more highbrow than Queen Elizabeth's.

Poor Martha liked Lincoln College but not Illinois winters. After a year she transferred to the University of Tampa.

• • •

The dorm directors and I had been hired by Lincoln's new president, J. Richard Stoltz. He had talked glowingly about the college's mission and how important it was for us to provide the leadership, order, and guidance the students needed to achieve their elusive potential. We were inspired.

He didn't tell us about the college's enrollment problems, or that the administration's goal seemed to be keeping most students enrolled, regardless of grades, behavior, or interests.

That policy would have a devastating effect on all of us.

We did have success stories, but like happy news items on television, they aren't as "newsworthy" or as memorable as the tragedies, the disasters, and the failures.

Most of the students went quietly about the business of learning and maturing.

Sometimes, though, even the successes elicited their own forms of guilt.

• • •

By April the dorm directors' morale was low, and their emotional exhaustion deemed complete.

A record year for vandalism and poor grades defined the school year. Barbara quit her position at Lincoln to teach psychology at a public community college fifty miles away, thus joining the other Lincolnites commuting long distances to work. Three other dorm directors moved out as soon as the year ended.

The dean had also soured on the dorms and created a new position—housing director—for me. I took the job because it was a challenge, because there was so much to do, and, I guess, because some idealism still lived in me.

• • •

My first goal as the new housing director was to hire good dorm directors and keep them—a real challenge, since I could only pay $2,000 plus room and board. Somehow, somewhere, I found them. Their only flaws were inexperience, but I knew that wouldn't last long.

I tried to give them more support and advice than Barbara and the others received the year before, but the results were mixed. Grades rose and vandalism decreased, but neither changed as much as we had hoped, and the emotional strain seemed as enormous as ever.

One new dorm director, Jean Gende, was slugged by a drunken student when she tried to break up a fight.

Jean also had a student, Alice, who suffered a psychotic reaction to LSD. When we found Alice, two of her friends were holding her in the shower trying to scrub paint off her body. An art major, Alice had taken tubes of paint and transformed her room, the hallway, and her body into a grotesque, abstract painting.

Alice babbled incoherently when we carried her from the shower, and she stayed that way. We took her to the hospital to make certain she wasn't overdosing. She wasn't, but her brain had seemingly turned to mush, clearly a bad reaction to the LSD. Jean finally had to call Alice's parents and tell them that—although the admissions office had promised to take their troubled young daughter and transform her into a well-adjusted college graduate— after only three months of campus life, she wasn't fit for more.

• • •

As the year ended, I felt that the dorm directors needed a chance to blow off a little steam. Barbara and I had them over to the old Madigan house for dinner and a little unique entertainment.

The idea came to me during our first spring in Lincoln at the college's annual awards ceremony.

Many of the awards were typical—the most valuable players of the athletic teams, best history student, highest grade point average, and so on.

Some, though, were pretty obscure. For example, the faculty was asked to vote for the student who best exemplified the ideals of the Boy Scouts—an award probably endowed by a long-forgotten alumnus.

The faculty judged the students by their behavior in the classroom and often voted awards without knowing anything about the students' out-of-class lifestyles. When the faculty voted the Boy Scout prize to a student who had had a loud, nasty argument with his gay lover the night before, I decided we needed our own awards.

The categories were for us, no one else. I created them

to help the dorm directors laugh and release some of their frustrations in a harmless way.

I invented awards such as the "Couple of the Year" for the romantic pair who had bothered us the most with their petty bickering and endless romantic crises. Another prize was for the student whose room was "Most Likely to Be Condemned by the Health Department."

The awards worked. Jean and the others ended the year on a happy note, and while the awards were never announced outside the dinner party, in our hearts, we knew.

The party worked that first year and became an annual event.

• • •

One of the awards announced at the party in the spring of 1975 was for the "Student Most Likely to Spend the Rest of His Life in Jail." The winner was a unanimous choice, a freshman from Joliet, Illinois, named Russell Smrekar.

I had had little personal contact with him during the year, but the dorm directors were convinced he was responsible for the huge increase in burglaries that had occurred on campus since his arrival.

I announced Smrekar as the winner, and we all nodded our heads. I went on to the next award, giving no more thought to Smrekar than to the kid with the messiest room. We liked to think his poor grades would discourage him from returning, although the college wouldn't flunk him out of school. We hoped we were finished with him.

Our troubles with Smrekar his freshman year were a picnic compared to what was to come. We would learn that our Lincoln education was not complete, after all.

Chapter III

There are burglaries on any campus, but they're not always reported. Occasionally a student might sell his stereo, claim it was stolen, then try to collect insurance money. Some thefts, usually of drugs, are not reported at all. And every campus has absent-minded students who lose a book or wallet and are convinced someone robbed them.

But the 1974-75 school year at Lincoln had an epidemic. Numerous dorm rooms were burglarized, some more than once. The dining hall and the student center were also robbed.

We were months into the school year before we realized some of the robberies followed the same frustrating pattern. They occurred during campus social events or a basketball game when the dorms were empty. The police and the dorm directors would question everyone involved and find nothing. No trace of the stolen items would ever be found.

When a Moog synthesizer was carried away through a second-floor window in the library, we realized we weren't dealing with the typical student thief who just wanted a little extra beer money.

We kept investigating, but we felt as effective as a rock thrown against a tank.

Eventually Len Branson, the dorm director for Carroll North Hall, told me Smrekar was the culprit.

I wasn't sure who Smrekar was. After Len described him to me, I vaguely remembered a tall, skinny white kid with long, unwashed hair. He was a loner with poor grades and apparently few friends.

I don't know what a professional burglar looks like, but Smrekar wasn't it. He looked too dopey—about as threatening as an ugly bug on my windshield.

But Len was convinced—and convincing. Every first-floor room in Carroll North that faced the alley had been robbed. Every room except Smrekar's.

Len also described the last time Smrekar joined a late-night bull session with other students on the floor. The students were talking about their idols—fathers, older brothers, rock stars, and athletes. Finally Smrekar said he most wanted to be like an older friend of his back in Joliet.

"What'd the guy do?" one of the students asked.

"Oh, it was a bitch. He got caught killing a guy, and now he's got a life sentence."

The other students looked at each other. The bull session broke up soon afterwards.

That's all the evidence Len had, and I wouldn't have paid much attention to it; however, Len was in his second year as a dorm director, and his judgment of a student's character had never been wrong.

If Len said Smrekar was guilty, then he probably was.

Knowing it was futile, I went to the Dean of Students and asked him to expel Smrekar. I admitted the case was weak, but I believed kicking Smrekar out of school was the only way to stop the robberies.

The Dean rejected the idea, of course. A school can't expel a student because of a dorm director's suspicions. By then the Dean had started a Judicial Board consisting of three faculty members, three students, and himself.

Even if he thought the evidence was enough, he said, the other board members wouldn't go for it.

Len and I decided we'd just have to work harder and find proof.

Soon after, another burglary was reported. Len searched Smrekar's room. Nothing.

The students' anger mounted as the thefts increased. One victim complained to me: "I can't go to a movie without gettin' my room ripped off? I came down here from a Chicago ghetto for this?"

Finally the year ended, and all we could do is award Smrekar our "Jail" award.

Maybe it wouldn't be us, we thought, but surely someone someday would catch him doing something.

Smrekar returned to Lincoln College in August of 1975 for his sophomore year. His grades had been lousy. We had hoped that the Academic Standards Committee would flunk him out, but his grades weren't as low as some other students' grade point averages, so they let him return.

At the time we wondered why he wanted to return. Surely there were places in Joliet he could rob if he truly was the professional thief we assumed he was. He hadn't received any scholarships, and he didn't have any die-hard friends on campus.

We all liked the town and the college, but we couldn't figure out why someone like Smrekar wanted to live among us.

We still don't know.

• • •

The burglaries began again in September of 1975. On a Thursday night, Barbara and I were attending a concert in the college theater with Debbie Blakely who had taken Jean Gende's dorm director job when Jean decided she'd been punched once too often.

Shortly after intermission, one of Debbie's residents, Diane, rushed up to us. Diane said she'd watched the first half of the concert, then returned to her room to find her guitar and her roommate's record albums stolen.

Debbie left the concert with Diane to call the police while I remained to pay the concert performers and close the theater.

By now the dorm directors knew the procedure: call the police, question the residents, and console the victims.

After the concert, some of the show organizers and I decided to buy the performers a beer. While I was walking to my car, Len Branson came up to me and said he'd just caught two of his residents with a strongbox that contained a pound of marijuana, a coded notebook, and $300.

Another eventful night at Lincoln College.

• • •

Waiting for me at my office the next morning were an FBI agent and three students holding some record albums. I had no waiting room, so everyone poured into the office when I opened the door. The students claimed their news was vital. I knew why the FBI agent was there, so I asked him to sit down and wait until I was finished with the others.

The agent was used to that. He would arrive on campus three or four times a year and ask about a student from Libya. Plane hijackings were making headlines around the world. Libya was officially classified as an unfriendly country, and, according to the agent, the FBI was responsible for checking all potential hijackers. Periodically the agent drove up from Springfield to ask about the Libyan student's political feelings and his travel plans.

Each time I would explain that this potential plane hijacker—all five-foot, five-inch, 125 pounds of him—had fallen in love with American women and American liquor. The Middle East could fall off the face of the earth for all he cared. He was too busy having a good time.

Apparently the agent was required to check in person, so he still came. He knew the routine, so he pulled up a chair in the corner and listened.

This time he had a lot to listen to.

The students gave me the albums. Many of them had the name, Joan Warner, scrawled on the jackets. Joan was Diane's roommate, and these albums had been stolen the night before.

The students said they'd caught one of their fellow residents of Carroll South Hall trying to dump the albums down the garbage chute early that morning.

News of the burglary had spread throughout the campus, and the students knew these albums were part of the crime.

I held the albums with mixed emotions. We finally had some evidence. Maybe now we could do something more than sympathize with the victim. During the investigations I had thought—hoped, really—that maybe there wasn't a cold, professional thief on campus. I preferred to think it just a few kids looking to rip off their insurance companies.

Now, however, I knew the burglaries were real. Rooms I'd never entered were broken into. Items I'd never seen were stolen by someone I didn't know. Someone was systematically, premeditatedly ripping off his classmates.

This thief was taking albums that kids hardly remembered they owned, cameras and books they needed for classes, stereos they couldn't afford to replace, and personal treasures the thief would sell for a few dollars.

The small size of the school made it worse. Someone ate in the dining hall and then stole a tape recorder from the kid who had probably passed him the salt. Someone danced with a girl in the student center and later broke into her room. Someone cheered a basketball player during the first half of a game and stole his stereo in the second half.

Robberies are robberies, I guess, whether the victim is an insurance company or a teenager. I realized, though, as I put the albums on my desk and called the police, I had been hoping it was the insurance companies. It felt less personal that way, perhaps less sinister.

● ● ●

The students reported they had caught Mike Mansfield with the albums. Mike was a sophomore honor student—quiet, almost painfully shy, and soft-spoken.

Mike Mansfield?

The students claimed Mike admitted getting the albums from Russ Smrekar shortly after the burglary. As the evening wore on, Mike claimed he became nervous about the albums and was getting rid of them when he was caught.

I called Smrekar's and Mike's dorm directors and asked them to find these guys and bring them to my office. One of the students left to look for Debbie, the dorm director.

Diane and Joan rushed into the office yelling that they'd heard about the recovery of the albums. They identified Joan's property and said now only the guitar was still missing. Diane started crying because her guitar was handmade and the most treasured possession she owned.

They were shocked to hear Mike might be involved. He was a friend of Joan's and had visited her room twice the previous week to hear these same albums.

The dorm directors walked into this conversation and told me Mike was in class.

According to Smrekar's roommate, Smrekar had left for Joliet for the weekend.

In the midst of all this, in walked Patti Davis, Smrekar's girlfriend. Without admitting she was involved, she said Smrekar left town when word spread about the burglary.

Then, two Carroll North residents came in and complained that Len Branson had no right to take their strongbox the night before.

By this time I had three dorm directors, three kids from Carroll South, two from Carroll North, Joan and Diane, and the FBI agent in my office. Everyone but the FBI agent was talking at once.

I finally told everyone to shut up. I informed the students from Carroll North that the police would be here shortly and proceeded to tell the students that they were welcome to ask the police about the marijuana in the strongbox.

I asked one of the dorm directors to go to Mike Mansfield's class and bring him to me when the class was over, and I asked everyone but the FBI agent to leave and return in fifteen minutes.

When everyone else was gone, I slumped in my chair and lit my fifth cigarette of the hour. The FBI agent pulled his chair closer to my desk and said, "Damn! You sure have an interesting job."

"Always willing to keep our public servants amused," I answered, as I reached for an ash tray.

Chapter IV

Mike Mansfield was still in class when the police arrived. They took Diane and Joan to the station with the albums and said they'd question Mike and Smrekar when he returned to campus from Joliet.

News spread about the burglaries, and students dropped in all morning. Victims asked if their possessions had been recovered, while others just volunteered to help.

Patti Davis returned with news that the guitar was now in Joliet. I'm not sure why she was being so helpful; she'd never been that way before. She seemed to be trying to get Smrekar off as lightly as possible.

She didn't care about the guitar or Smrekar's victims. She was just helping her boyfriend out of a jam. There was never a question of dropping a lover because he was a thief; he just got caught, that's all.

Florence Molen, an elderly English professor, visited me between students. There wasn't a more prim-and-proper individual on campus, and she had tears in her eyes. "Mike couldn't have done those things," she pleaded. "He's just too nice a young man."

I told her I didn't know all of the facts myself and was trying to withhold judgment until I talked to Mike.

"Well, if he needs a character witness or anything else for the Judicial Board," she added as she rose to leave. "I'll be proud to speak for him. He's my best student in my Shakespeare class, and you tell him that, please."

Two other students came in that morning to report that Smrekar had been stealing from stores in Joliet and selling the items on campus. Record albums in particular, they said, because they still had the K-Mart label on them. Smrekar had been selling them for over a year to students.

"How could you buy something you knew was stolen?"

"I dunno," they answered in tandem.

"Here were all these burglaries in your dorm; how could you encourage a chronic thief like that? If he was stealing from Joliet on weekends, did it not occur to you that he might steal from you during the week?"

"I just thought he stole from other people."

Both students seemed to share the same attitude. If it didn't affect them, apparently, it was okay.

• • •

As the rumors spread and the students became angrier, I thought it best to talk to Mike in his room, away from the fishbowl environment of my office.

We talked for a long time that Friday afternoon. The sun went down, yet neither of us thought to turn on a light. As he talked, Mike seemed to almost fade before my eyes in the gathering darkness.

What emerged was a kid who inadvertently became involved with a criminal. Once he realized his friend was a thief, he was too frightened to act, until he became too frightened not to. He said he went along with Smrekar giving him albums and electronics to hold for him until this latest burglary: Mike saw Diane's name on the albums, and Diane was a friend of Mike's.

That was too much. He didn't know what else to do, so he tried to dump the albums in the dorm trash chute, and he was caught by other students.

The day before, Mike was a successful college student—the kind whose parents would thank me at graduation. He was in the student honor society; he was a reliable and popular disc jockey on the college's new radio station; most importantly, he was well-liked, if not well known by his peers.

Now he was a sad, frightened, skinny kid whose dreams were fading with the sunlight.

He was in more trouble than he'd ever been in his life, and he knew it.

Sounding like a priest in a confessional, I told Mike this wasn't the end of the world. If he was honest with the police and me about Smrekar, I'd recommend probation to the college's Judicial Board and ask the police to go easy with him.

He agreed and related essentially the same story he'd told the students who had found him with the albums. Then he went to his closet and gave me two CB radios Smrekar had given him to "take care of for a while."

Finally it was time for Mike to work at the radio station, the one place where he seemed to overcome his shyness.

After he left, I sat there in the darkness for a few moments, wondering how it all happened and if the students—and Florence Molen—would accept him again.

I left Mike's room and listened to him on the car radio as I drove home. He sounded nervous, but he went on with the show.

• • •

The anger in Smrekar's dorm grew through the weekend. So much so that Len was frightened by what the residents might do if Smrekar were left alone.

To protect him—and other students from getting in trouble because they might administer a little dorm-style justice—Len waited in the dorm's study lounge all day Sunday for Smrekar to appear. He could see Smrekar's door from the lounge, and when Smrekar did return, Len ordered him to stay in his room with the door locked.

The police had told us to call as soon as Smrekar returned, but I wanted to talk to him first. I knew once the police were involved, he'd never admit he had Diane's guitar. On that Indian summer afternoon, Len called me instead of the police. As I drove to campus, I waved hello to a half dozen friends and neighbors who were working on their lawns and barbecuing Sunday dinner. The smell of burning leaves mixed with the aroma of townsfolk enjoying one last cookout before winter.

On campus, students were chucking footballs and tossing frisbees in front of the dorms. A co-ed football game was going on across the street from Smrekar's dorm, and I could hear the shrieks of laughter from the participants. As I got out of my car, a couple of them invited me to join, but I declined.

"What's the matter, Mike? Don't you want to tackle these girls?"

"That's not it," I replied. "If I tackled anybody, you'd yell 'administration brutality.'"

They laughed and returned to their game—except one, who yelled, "Mr. Hartnett, if you're lookin' for Len, he's upstairs in Smrekar's room." Then he too went back to football.

The shouts faded as I climbed the stairs to the second floor and thought about the confrontation waiting for me.

I was going to be nice first, but if that didn't work, I was ready with another plan.

Educators are daily faced with trying to change students' anti-social or self-defeating behavior. Normal counseling techniques or threats of discipline usually succeeded, but once a year or so, I'd hit a stone wall. The counseling wouldn't work, and the college administration wouldn't do more than give a slap on the wrist; however, the behavior had to change.

When I found myself between a rock and a hard place, I'd draw upon some actor's training I'd received in college to build myself into a rage. I called it my Technique of Last Resort. I'd erupt and appear on the verge of losing control—yelling and swearing at the student. The act always worked. The student either became so frightened of me that he'd stop the behavior, or he'd become so angry that he'd stop the behavior just to show me.

I didn't learn this technique in graduate school, and I never liked it; however, it worked, and I could never think of a better substitute.

• • •

When I walked into the room, Len was sitting at the desk, and Smrekar was lying on his bed propped up on his elbows. It was one of the dullest dorm rooms I had ever seen. No attempt had been made to decorate, make it homey or personal.

I pulled a chair next to the bed and sat down. Choosing to keep the Attila-the-Hun act in my back pocket, I figured it would be a good idea to start on a softer foot. "Russ, we wanted to talk to you privately about what's going on here over the weekend while you were gone."

"What?"

"Mike Mansfield got caught with the record albums from the Hoyle burglary Thursday night. He said he got the records from you."

"So? I didn't give him no records."

"Russ, it's over. Mike told me the whole story about that robbery and all the others you've pulled on campus. And he's planning to tell the police."

"I don't know nothing."

"Russ, the police ordered us to call them as soon as you got back here, but we wanted to talk to you first to try and help. There will be a Judiciary Board hearing this week for you and Mike, and it looks bad.

"The campus is really pissed. That's why Len was sitting in the study lounge waiting for you. He was afraid you'd be in danger from the other guys in the dorm."

"For what?" he asked me, blankly looking at my face without emotion or remorse.

"The students are blaming you for every robbery since you've been here. They're really mad, and we're not sure it's safe for you."

"I can take care of myself."

"Russ, I only see one way out. You've got to cooperate. I think the J-Board will throw you out of school, but it's the police I'm worried about. You've made them look like fools with all the robberies, and they're mad. You've got to cooperate, or they may throw the book at you."

"What do you mean?"

"You've got to tell us where the guitar is."

"No, I don't."

God, his eyes were so cold.

"Russ, this is serious. The students are already mad as hell, and Diane is walking around like you stole her closest friend. If you give back the guitar, it will at least show everybody you're sorry. It's the only way you can convince the police to go easy."

"I don't know anything about no guitar."

The son of a bitch was barely listening to me, just staring back at me with his cold, cold eyes. It was time for plan B, Attila the Hun. I got up and walked to the window.

I turned and shouted an obscene tirade at Smrekar, who laid calmly on his bed. I told him the guys in the dorm were so mad, if he didn't tell us where the guitar was, we'd sit back and let them beat the shit out of him.

As if on cue, two students burst through the door I'd forgotten to lock. They were carrying baseball bats. "All right, motherfucker, do I beat your ass with this bat, or do you tell me where my goddamn camera is that you stole last year?"

Smrekar just shrugged.

"Hey, asshole, I asked you a question!" the student yelled as he raised the bat. Len grabbed the bat and pushed the two out the door.

I was standing over Smrekar, who hadn't moved.

"YOU SEE THAT, YOU LITTLE SHIT! THAT WAS NO GODDAMN ACT. YOU CAN TAKE YOUR DIP-SHIT DENIALS AND SHOVE 'EM UP YOUR ASS, BECAUSE NOBODY IS GOING TO BELIEVE YOU. NOT ME, NOT THE GUYS IN THE DORM, NOT THE J-BOARD, AND SURE AS HELL NOT THE POLICE!"

"I'll get out of it."

That started me on another obscene tirade, to no avail.

"I'll be all right."

"Well, fuck it," I finally relented. "Len, go call the police."

• • •

Sometime during the confrontation, Smrekar began to frighten me. I don't know when, but after I left the room, I began to tremble.

I'd never seen eyes like those. Deep and empty and ice cold. No fear, no anger, nothing. Smrekar lay there on his bed and stared right through me as if I were talking a foreign language.

Nothing I said had mattered to him. The baseball bats hadn't frightened him. He took in the threats, the anger, and the implied violence calmly, as if he was watching a rerun of Seinfeld. What we said and did had no more effect on him than a fly buzzing around his head. The look in his eyes told me he wasn't concerned at all about the idea of consequences for his actions.

I left the dorm and drove home, still trembling.

Chapter V

The Judicial Board met the following Wednesday in the board room in University Hall. It wasn't called the board room for us, but for the college board of directors, and the room was kept locked when they weren't meeting. The dean had suggested we use the room for our meetings though, hoping the huge, felt-covered table, tall ceiling, and oaken walls would instill a little more respect for the board than we had inspired on our own.

None of us wanted to play the campus tough guy, and the students knew it. The students weren't frightened of the board, but they were a little awe-struck when they entered the room. The first witnesses, the Carroll South students who found Mike with the albums, thought the room was wonderful and after they'd answered my questions, asked if the student senate could use the room for a party someday.

The mood was light-hearted during their testimony. The students were telling their story to friends and only worried that Mike would get in trouble.

But the mood changed quickly when the students left, and Mike slowly entered the room. The tension seemed to ooze from him, mixed with the smell of cigarette smoke, and hung heavy in the air.

As the "prosecutor," I usually had to ask a number of questions to the student witnesses to pry their knowledge out of them. This time, all I needed to say was, "Okay, Mike, tell us what you know."

Mike spoke quietly with his hands clasped tightly and his head bowed. Students testifying at board hearings sometimes avoided eye contact because they weren't being entirely truthful, and they knew it.

Not Mike. He just seemed ashamed.

Occasionally a board member would ask Mike to speak up when his fragile voice didn't carry across the long table. He told his story as he told it to me, but this time he couldn't hide his embarrassment behind a setting sun. The board was quiet when Mike left the room—quiet in the way people are when they overhear something embarrassing.

Now it was time for my part of the bargain. I told the board Mike deserved another chance in light of his stellar record at Lincoln and his cooperation with us. Most students would be too embarrassed to stay, I said. The fact Mike wanted to remain was a sign that a college education was genuinely important to him. All the board members, including the students, agreed.

No one wanted to expel Mike, despite his actions and despite the criticism the board would receive from those who only knew the facts and did not witness Mike's awkward, wretched testimony.

Mike was allowed to stay in school on probation. The dean called him back into the room and warned him that any kind of future violation of a campus regulation would mean expulsion, but I knew that wouldn't be a problem. Mike had learned his lesson.

• • •

Next it was Smrekar's turn. The board had a reputation for leniency with students, and I was afraid something would happen to ruin the case against him. My fears increased when Smrekar entered the room—confident, nonchalant, and flashing a rare smile.

I needn't have worried. Smrekar testified on his own behalf and destroyed any possible chance he had of staying in school. The three student board members took the lead in questioning him and trapped him in contradictions three times.

After a few minutes, it seemed each question began with "Now, wait a minute. You just said the opposite of what you're saying now . . ."

Ironically, there was little hard evidence against him. The case essentially was Mike's word against Smrekar's—until he testified. He made such a mess of his own case that he removed any doubt the board members may have had.

But Smrekar remained calm during his testimony, even as he was caught lying. He looked us all in the eye and offered his silly lies so matter-of-factly that I wondered later if he realized how absurd his story sounded.

He wasn't angry, worried, or nervous. And despite his claim of cooperation with the board, he wasn't truthful.

When Smrekar finished and left the room, the board voted quickly and conclusively. It was rare the board ever voted unanimously, but in this case no one had any doubt of Smrekar's guilt.

The dean called him back into the room and told him the verdict. Smrekar didn't blink. When asked if he had any statement before the board determined the penalty, Smrekar answered pleasantly, "Well, if you have any more questions, I'll be happy to answer 'em."

It was as if he hadn't heard the guilty verdict, and he still thought a few more lies would somehow save him.

"No, Russell," the dean answered, puzzled. "We've already asked our questions and found you guilty. Is there anything you want to say, anything we should consider while we decide the punishment?"

"Like I said," Smrekar replied, still calm and objective. "If you have any questions, just ask."

We exchanged puzzled looks as Smrekar left the room.

"What the hell's wrong with that guy?" one board member asked.

"Who knows?" answered another. "Let's just get him outta here."

"I second the motion."

"Moved and seconded. Any discussion? Okay, vote on a piece of paper and give it to me," the dean said quickly.

The members voted immediately and gave the papers to the dean.

"It's yes. Bring him back in."

Smrekar listened without emotion to the decision that he was being expelled.

"Do you have anything to say?" Bowers asked him.

"Well, like I said before, I'll be happy to answer any questions."

He still didn't get the point. Dean Bowers looked at the other Judicial Board members and shook his head. "No Russell. We've asked more than enough. Be off campus in twenty-four hours."

Smrekar shrugged and rose. As he and I left the room, he stopped in the doorway, turned, and tapped me on the chest with his finger. "You know, Hartnett, I'm gonna drop out of this school tomorrow."

Drop out?

"Russ," I said slowly, "you're not *in* school anymore.

You can't drop out of it if you're not in it."

"Oh."

He left campus that evening, driving, we assumed, back to his mother's house in Joliet, about a hundred miles from Lincoln.

• • •

Two days after the Judicial Board hearing, I received a phone call from a friend on the police force.

"Hey, Hartnett," he said jubilantly, "guess who we just busted for shoplifting at the Kroger store?"

Here we go again. "I know, I know. Some L.C. student."

"No, no, no, an ex-L.C. student."

"Who?"

"Smrekar! The jerk was walkin' out with a couple pieces of meat. The manager and his assistant saw him and chased him out in the parking lot. Smrekar threw the meat under what he thought was a parked car, 'cept it wasn't an empty car. Woman named Ruth Martin had just pulled up and saw Smrekar throw the meat under her car. The dumb shit."

"I don't get it," I told my happy friend. "What the hell was he still doin' in town, anyway? He hasn't been on campus, or I would have heard of it."

"I dunno what he was doing, but one thing's for sure, we really got 'em now. The burglary case looks good, and there are three witnesses to this shoplifting. He's finished."

• • •

Life went on at dear old Lincoln College. The campus seemed to breathe easier for a moment with Smrekar gone, but soon the inevitable day-to-day crises of getting an education and growing up took over, and Smrekar was almost forgotten.

Mike remained in school and continued as he had been—quiet, shy, but accepted. Kids are always surprising educators; that's why so many of us stay in the profession, despite the pay. The Lincoln kids were wonderful to Mike, treating him as if his association with Smrekar was a temporary aberration of his character, which it was.

The police investigations continued, but they did not affect us; most of the investigations were unknown by most of the campus. The police believed Smrekar was the mastermind of the dorm burglaries, but they only had Mike's word for it. The police asked both Mike and Smrekar to take lie detector tests, and Mike agreed.

In a surprise to all of us, so did Smrekar. When Patti Davis told me Smrekar was convinced he could fool the machine, pass the test, and beat the charges, I thought back to his comment to me, "I'll get out of it." Apparently he still thought that way.

The first set of tests were inconclusive, and both agreed to take them again. This time, according to the police, Smrekar flunked. Apparently the key question was, "Do you know where the guitar is now?" Smrekar said no, the machine said yes, and the police were convinced.

Soon after the tests, the Joliet police recovered the guitar. Patti told me, without any embarrassment, that she thought the guitar was in the house of Smrekar's "hometown" girlfriend, who shared Smrekar with Patti. The information was relayed to the Joliet police who were given the guitar by the girl's mother.

The Lincoln police kept the guitar for evidence, and now the case really was finished.

Chapter VI

I guess it would have been easy to interpret what happened in the next seven months as omens of the future—almost like signposts on the way to some horrible destination.

But we didn't. We thought we had caught a professional thief and sent him out of our lives; that justice did, in fact, prevail. Each event that occurred after Smrekar left campus was seen as the last of him, if connected to him at all.

He was only a thief, wasn't he? A strange one, perhaps, but schools are always filled with unusual people. Smrekar seemed no more unusual, in his own way, than the character who loved to visit women in the bathroom. At the time, far more concern was given to our peeping Tom because he was still on campus, and he still needed help we couldn't give him, and Smrekar was, we thought, long gone.

• • •

Another day and another phone call from my friendly neighborhood police officer.

"Hartnett, you should see Smrekar's record. Jesus Christ, this guy's done just about everything but rape and murder. How the hell could you let a guy like that in school?"

"What do you want from us," I answered, tired of townspeople complaining that we let so many "weirdos" on campus.

"Should we put a question in our admission application asking if they'd committed any crimes lately?

"And whaddya think they'd answer, 'Oh yes sir, I stole four cars last month, but please accept me anyway'? Do you think we *plan* it this way, that we go around to Chicago street gangs and say, 'Gee fellas, here's a scholarship'? Colleges can't do criminal background checks on every student who applies."

"Well, ya shoulda kicked him out sooner," the policeman grumbled.

"Yeah, I know, but it's easier said than done."

• • •

Weeks went by before I read in the local paper that Smrekar's burglary trial was postponed. The state's attorney had asked for, without explanation, a delay.

Now it was my turn to call the police. It seemed someone had broken into the police station—or snuck in, the police didn't know which—gone to the detective's squad room where evidence is kept for pending trials, and stolen Joan's albums and Diane's guitar.

That sounds bizarre, but having seen the police station, I knew it could happen. Open the front door and there's a staircase ahead and a door to the left. The top half of the door was usually open, like a window, and the stairs led up to the evidence lockers. If it were late at night and no one was at the door, the thief could sneak under the window, climb the stairs, and check the evidence lockers.

The police had no doubt who robbed them, but they had no evidence either. There was no sign of forced entry and no fingerprints, only a menacing calling card: the culprit apparently had not wished to be disturbed as he fumbled through the evidence lockers because he had taken a shotgun out of another locker, loaded it, and placed it on a nearby desk, pointed in the direction of the room's only door.

Diane would not see her precious guitar again.

• • •

I had heard students say they never felt quite the same about their dorm room after it had been broken into. Somehow, they said, the room had been violated; it just wasn't "clean" anymore.

Now it had happened to the police station. I had developed a fondness for the silly old building, maybe because it seemed so appropriate for the town.

It wasn't big, fancy, or frightening. Hell, those were our *friends* working in there, ready to help out. Many of them had attended special schools to learn modern police techniques, but when a bad summer storm came, one of them still had to go up on the roof to watch for tornados. And if he saw anything, he would use the world's only working telephone booth situated on a police station roof and phone down a warning before scampering to safety.

The creaky old structure was small and served as the official meeting place for the city council. There wasn't much room in the building, so when the police conducted a lineup, everyone would march into the empty council chambers for the event.

Lineups posed a special problem for the police. There were never enough officers on duty who matched the general description of the accused, so the police had to look elsewhere. The fire station next door never had many people on duty, so that wasn't the answer. And townspeople off the street were probably known by the witness, the accused, the police, and the victim, so they weren't the answer either.

Usually I was the answer. "Uh, Mike, this is Tom at the station. Could you get us four or five guys about five-ten with light brown hair and bring 'em down about three this afternoon?"

I'd find the appropriate students who didn't have a three o'clock class and drive them downtown to the city council chambers. The kids thought it was a grand adventure for justice.

Now the building itself had been broken into, raped, and some of its most important contents—per the students—snatched away. The kids were right; it wasn't the same anymore. Every time I sat in the detectives' squad room after the burglary, I would think about that shotgun resting menacingly on a desk.

• • •

The fall semester passed uneventfully. It contained the usual quota of joyous "Prayer Meetings," frightening tests, lovers' quarrels, loud dances, drunken fights, painful realizations, tearful counseling sessions, boring faculty meetings, long hours, low pay, stimulating rap sessions, and probably some other things I'd rather not have known about.

It was a community of people, each playing their part. The old college, chronically short of money, lumbered and creaked its way towards graduation when it would send part of itself out into the world a little smarter and, hopefully, a little wiser.

Everybody's actions were familiar and within context; the students and faculty acted like students and faculty, warts and all. We'd complain about the top administrators, but that was typical of most colleges.

Mike blended back into his dorm and classes, and his radio voice regained the confidence that had been lacking for a while.

Patti Davis dropped out of school to be with her true love, I assumed, wherever he was.

• • •

I guess there was a special event that fall. Special to me, anyway.

The basketball team had begun to play and promised to be coach Al Pickering's most exciting team in years.

As was typical at Lincoln, Al and his assistant had to do it all. There was no money to pay a trainer, official scorer, public address announcer, or statisticians; there was no one to organize ticket sales, concessions, or publicity. Al did everything himself or charmed his friends into helping out.

Barb and I were two of the charmed, and we'd go to each game early for our "assignments."

"Mike, Danny can't make it tonight. Could you be the PA announcer *and* run the score-board?"

The away games were a little different. Barbara and I would drive to such garden spots as Mattoon, Olney, and Robinson, usually with a business teacher, Dave Daniel—whose nickname was "The Big Bopper"—and a few students. Dave would be the official scorer, while the rest of us would keep stats and cheer. I would call a summary of the game into the area newspapers, and Al would buy us hamburgers when it was over.

But during the Thanksgiving break that year, Al had a problem. The team was playing in a tournament in Kewanee, and the students and Dave Daniel were home visiting their parents.

Barb and I made the two-hour drive each way on Friday night to keep stats on Lincoln's victory, but Saturday night, the championship game, would be a different story. It was our anniversary, and I didn't have the courage to ask Barb to give up our planned romantic evening in order to spend four hours in a car to watch sweating teenagers throw a ball through a hoop.

We ran into Al at Gem Lunch that Saturday morning and over a typically enormous Pete Andrews breakfast, we broke the news to him.

Al was his charming, gracious, devious self. He said of course we shouldn't go to the game, even though it promised to be tremendously exciting, and while he had absolutely no one else to keep stats, he would struggle along—somehow. Then he paid for our breakfasts.

I didn't say a word about the game while we ran our Saturday morning errands. Finally, as we were driving back to the old Madigan house, Barb spoke up.

"We're going to dinner and a movie tonight, right?"

"Yeah."

"What did you have planned for my birthday next week?"

"Oh, I thought we'd do it again, go to dinner and a movie."

"Hmmm." She followed with silence.

A moment later she asked, "Ya know, we could sort of combine the two, do them next week, and go to the game tonight?"

No wonder I married that woman.

So we drove to the game, watched Al laugh uproariously when we entered the gym, and kept stats for one of the most exciting games I have ever seen.

Lincoln won by a few points in double overtime after five players on the other team fouled out of the game.

When the game was finally over, Barb and I were busily totaling the statistics and did not watch the awards presentation. We were almost finished with the rebounds, assists, and points when a young voice asked,

"Uh, Mr. and Mrs. Harnett?"

We looked up, and there was the team surrounding us in the grandstand, all smiles. This sweaty, joyous bunch of winners said "Happy Anniversary" in unison and showed us the trophy.

Walking out of the gym that night, after phoning in the game to the papers and just beating the janitor out the door, I thought to myself, "Dammit, I want to stay at Lincoln College forever."

Chapter VII

The spring semester began in early January of 1976 with the usual number of problems. Rookies replaced those who graduated at midterm, while the old pros negotiated for the few single rooms available in the dorms. Others pleaded with us for relief from roommates who had driven them crazy during the fall.

The first few days saw the dorm directors and I playing an elaborate chess game. "Let's see, if we move Johnson out of 106 like he wants, then Shapstein will get a single room because nobody else will move in with him. Then Fluker will bitch because he's ahead of Shapstein on the waiting list for single rooms . . .We have to move our Libyan friend closer to his dorm director so he can keep an eye on his drinking, and if we don't move Holloway he'll die from his roommate's cigar smoke . . .."

By the second week of the semester, the jigsaw puzzle was almost complete when the dorm director for Carroll South came into my office.

"Mike, is Mansfield coming back?"

"Whattya mean coming back? Isn't he here?"

"Nope. His stuff is gone too, but that doesn't mean anything. I told all my kids to take everything home. We've had enough robberies, and I didn't want anything stolen over vacation. But he hasn't come back. Should I use his room for someone else?"

I told him to wait. We always had a few students who strolled onto campus minutes before late registration ended and said, "Oh, am I late?" Mike Mansfield didn't seem the type to do that, but you never knew what was going on at home. Sometimes the latecomers would feign ignorance to cover a family crisis that made it impossible for them to arrive earlier.

The end of the week came, but Mike didn't, and his room, where we had talked until dusk, was given away.

I checked with the admissions and dean's offices, but no one had been notified Mike was not returning. His first semester grades were fine; he had no reason to quit school out of anger or a sense of failure.

Mike's absence from campus seemed ominous, out of character, and the old questions returned. This was a common burglary, wasn't it? And then the memory of Smrekar's cold, flat eyes would slither through the images of the past few months and present itself in front of my brain.

I'd think to myself, "I gotta find out about this," but then another student would come in the office with a problem that wouldn't wait, then another student, and another, and the day would be gone.

Problems that wouldn't wait usually meant counseling a pregnant girl, investigating a fight in the dorms the night before, booking a band for next month's dance, encouraging two roommates to really talk to each other, asking maintenance why a dorm shower hadn't been fixed, arranging for busses to a basketball tournament, talking to the student senate president about his next senate meeting, and trying to help some kid decide whether to continue his schooling after graduation or join the family business.

Soon it would be five o'clock, and as I'd hurry home to eat before returning to campus for a student activity, I'd realize another day had passed without having checked on Mike. And the uneasiness would return.

A month passed. I was sitting at my desk one cold February day when two friends of Mike's rushed in.

"Did you know Mike's really disappeared?"

"Mike who? You mean Mansfield?"

"Yeah. Mrs. Mansfield called and said no one knows where Mike is. She said Mike left home in Rolling Meadows [a Chicago suburb] on New Year's Eve, and nobody's seen him since."

Mike was really gone.

What the hell is going on here? Do you run away from what was probably a normal home, give up a promising college career, and hide from your friends because of someone's eyes? They were frightening, but Christ, so are a lot of things in life.

Then I started rationalizing. There had to be more to it than I knew. Maybe things went to hell at home, and Mike left, knowing he couldn't return to school or his parents would find him there. Maybe his repentance was a bluff to keep him in college through the semester and he had no intention of testifying against Smrekar. Maybe he just panicked and fled, too frightened to stay and now too scared to return.

I didn't know the answer. But after the students left, I sat in my office and thought about him: a shy teenager out there, somewhere, probably on the run, with no job or experience except introducing rock 'n roll records.

I called Mrs. Mansfield, and she told me essentially the same story I'd heard from Mike's friends. Mike had a phone call the afternoon of New Year's Eve. He talked for a few minutes, then took his jacket and said he'd be gone "about an hour." She had not seen him since then.

As we talked, I eliminated family problems as a primary motive for Mike's leaving home. Mrs. Mansfield sounded like a very nice, very worried mother who just wanted her boy safe and happy. Like a good mother was supposed to, she had sent her son to college in pursuit of the American Dream. Eighteen months later she was confronted with burglary, state's attorneys, police, a college judicial board, and her boy was gone.

Now she seemed to be saying to hell with the American Dream, the police and all that; let's just get my boy back home.

I didn't cancel the family problem theory altogether, though, because some parents are excellent at presenting one image of family life to educators, while the truth is something quite different. But Mrs. Mansfield sure didn't sound like someone Mike would want to run away from.

• • •

A week later, Mike's friends returned to my office. "You remember Thelma Patterson, who graduated in January and transferred to Eureka College? She was probably Mike's closest friend on campus, and she thinks she may have heard from him."

"*May* have heard? What do you mean?"

"Well, she got a post card recently from someone who signed his name, 'The Wanderer.' Whoever wrote it said he was just traveling around. We can't imagine Mike would hit the road like that, and he never used the name 'Wanderer' before, but Thelma can't think of anybody else who'd write those things to her."

"What about the handwriting? Is it Mike's?"

"She thinks it is, but she doesn't know for sure. He never wrote to her much, but she said it looks kinda familiar. Mr. Hartnett, what the hell is all this?"

"I wish I knew."

• • •

In early March, as the campus recovered from the basketball team's loss in the sectional tournament, the police called again.

"Mike, any word about the Mansfield kid?"

"Nothing definite. A friend of his who transferred to Eureka got a card she thinks may have been written by him, but she's not sure. Why?"

"Because the state's attorney has issued a warrant for his arrest."

"What for? I thought the charges against him were dropped because he said he'd testify against Smrekar."

"Yeah, but he didn't. The hearing was January 5, and Mansfield never showed."

"Of course he didn't show. That was five days after he disapp . . . January 5? Holy shit, you mean he disappeared just before he was supposed to testify?"

"That's right, friend. The state's attorney had to get a postponement. We're calling the Rolling Meadows police to see what they know. But keep an eye out for him, and let us know if you or any of the students see him."

"Yeah. See ya."

I sat at my desk, stunned.

Then a student came in, red faced and fire in his eyes. "Mr. Hartnett, what are we going to do about my roommate? I can't stand it anymore!"

Back to the here and now, forgetting about Mike's disappearance altogether.

• • •

Later that month Mike's friends returned to my office with a letter they'd received from Mike's mother. Mrs. Mansfield had just been told that there was a warrant for Mike's arrest, as if she didn't have enough to worry about.

In her letter she expressed the fear we all had in the back of our minds.

> *In some way, I feel he might have been threat-*
> *ened if he testified, and that could be why he left*
> *home and school. If that's the reason, the longer*
> *he stays away, the harder it's going to be on him.*

She went on, saying she wanted to talk to Diane, whose records Mike was once again accused of stealing.

Joan and Diane were still distraught over the robbery, and they certainly didn't need to talk to a mother who was more distraught than they were.

I called the police and explained Mrs. Mansfield's fears. The Lincoln police were essentially powerless because Mike disappeared from Rolling Meadows, which was outside their jurisdiction.

They did say if Mike returned and explained that he ran away out of fear, then the state's attorney would probably still avoid prosecuting him—if he'd come home. I also explained there was no need for Mike's mom to talk to Diane and Joan.

We promised to keep in touch.

• • •

Smrekar and Patti Davis returned to Lincoln in early April for a hearing on the meat-shoplifting charge. While

Smrekar was in court, Patti paid me a visit and denied knowledge of Mike's disappearance. She acted as if she had no idea Mike was gone, although she must have known since the state's attorney had asked for another postponement in January.

She denied everything, wearing that miserable, leering grin of hers.

• • •

About a week later, Thelma returned to Lincoln with a letter that seemed to change everything.

It apparently had the same handwriting as "The Wanderer" card, but this was signed "The Wanderer and Disco." Thelma had called Mike "Disco" because of his radio experience.

Although the card was postmarked to Rockford, a city not far from Rolling Meadows, the writer said he wasn't in Rockford but would be coming home soon.

The letter relieved a lot of tension for me personally, far more than I realized I was holding. Mike had taken off, and we were back to looking at common burglary again.

Coincidently, Thelma said she was shopping in Eureka the previous week, and she spotted Smrekar in the dime store. Eureka, a four-year version of Lincoln College and Ronald Reagan's alma mater, was about seventy miles from Lincoln—and thirty miles from the interstate highway connecting Lincoln and Smrekar's home in Joliet.

Thelma said Smrekar looked at her curiously, as if to say, "Don't I know you?" She left the store quickly without talking to him. She was frightened. Why was he in Eureka? Was he going to threaten her? Maybe Smrekar was "The Wanderer?"

I had no answers to her questions, but it all seemed insignificant against the fact that Mike was apparently all right. He was in Eureka. There may have been harmless reasons he was there. Many Lincoln students who enjoyed the college's small, intimate atmosphere—and who had any money left after two years of a private college—would transfer to Eureka after graduation. Perhaps Smrekar was visiting some other Lincoln alumnus.

Whatever the case, I really believed that Mike would surely be heading home to his mother. I immediately called Mrs. Mansfield, but there was no answer. I had to share my relief with her somehow, so I wrote to her. Part of the letter said:

"Thelma was uncertain about calling you—she said that she was afraid that it might upset you more. I told her I was positive you would want to know about it—so at least you would know Mike was alive and well."

Mrs. Mansfield wrote back quickly, ending the letter with the first sign of happiness I'd seen from her since Mike had disappeared:

"I am very optimistic that I will hear from my son soon, and nothing would make a nicer Mother's Day gift but to hear from Mike."

There were still lots of unanswered questions, as there often are with students. But none of them mattered anymore. I had convinced myself that Mike was coming home.

• • •

But Mike did not come home. Mother's Day and graduation passed by without Mrs. Mansfield receiving the gift she had hoped for so badly.

I kept assuming Mike was all right and had just left home in a particularly unkind way. I was disappointed and felt I had overestimated him. That had happened with students before, though, and would again. Ultimately it was his life and his decision, which was fine, but how could he do that to his mother?

A month later, I was putting the finishing touches on my year-end report and next year's budget request when the phone rang.

"Mike, this is Tom down at the station. I've got an agent here from the Illinois Bureau of Investigation, and we'd like to come over and talk."

I started to laugh. "Talk about what? Tom, the kids went home three weeks ago; there's NOBODY here. What the hell is there to talk about, besides the White Sox?"

"Ruth Martin."

"Ruth Martin? You mean the real estate lady who disappeared a couple weeks ago?"

"Yeah."

"Well, sure, come over. But what do you want to talk to me for? I only met her once a few months ago when she showed Barb and me a couple of houses."

"She's one of the witnesses in the shoplifting case against Smrekar."

• • •

Ruth Martin disappeared from her home on June 2, 1976, where the police found blood stains on the floor of her empty garage. Days later, in the parking lot of a Holiday Inn in Bloomington, thirty miles to the north, they discovered her car with blood stains in the trunk.

Chapter VIII

Ruth was a middle-aged real estate agent, mother, and wife. She wasn't a leader; she didn't make news. She was just a nice, friendly, ordinary woman who went about her life quietly.

One evening eight months earlier, she had driven to the local Kroger store for groceries. As she pulled into a parking lot, turned off the ignition, and shut off the lights, she saw a young man running out of the store with small packages under his arm.

He was followed by two shouting store employees. He ran towards her car and threw the packages under it, apparently not realizing she was sitting there in the dark watching him.

She kept watching as the employees caught the skinny, bedraggled-looking character. One of the employees crawled under her car and retrieved the packages—pieces of meat the young man had stolen from the store.

Then she got out of her car and confronted the surprised shoplifter, Russ Smrekar.

• • •

The Lincoln detectives said they didn't think Smrekar had anything to do with Ruth Martin's disappearance, but they had investigated every other lead and come up with nothing; only that Ruth was probably dead because of the amount of blood on her garage floor and in the trunk of her car. They even brought in an agent from the Illinois Bureau of Investigation for advice. They were checking the Smrekar connection because they had nowhere else to turn.

The IBI agent asked me to tell the Smrekar saga from the beginning. As I told the story, I edited out all the intervening details of campus life—and my life—that had so distracted me from paying complete attention to this albatross that would not go away.

I talked about the burglaries but not the basketball games; Smrekar's calm, cold indifference to school rules but not the prayer meetings; the stolen evidence but not the crying girls; Mrs. Mansfield and Thelma but not roommate problems and the drunken Libyan.

When I plucked the Smrekar details out of their daily context and reported them in order, they painted a grim, threatening picture. They made the case much more ominous than I had ever allowed myself to consider.

The police finally left, unconvinced Smrekar was the key. They had no jurisdiction with Mike's disappearance in Rolling Meadows, and they had no evidence. Russ was charged with stealing a couple of pieces of meat. Even if the shoplifting conviction would have meant prison, surely he wouldn't kill someone over a piece of steak?

● ● ●

As much as Barbara and I liked small-town living, we were unprepared for the effects of small-town crime. We grew up learning from the *Chicago Tribune* that violence was all around us all the time, although no one we knew ever died from it.

But we knew Ruth Martin, and all our friends knew her, too.

A woman who spends her life in a small town touches almost everyone living there. An ordinary person doing the ordinary things—working, raising a family, going to church—becomes a variation of a celebrity in a small-town way and achieves a fame that no one notices until she is plucked out of that ordinary life, leaving the rest of us to notice the gap her absence makes.

One reason people live in a small town is for protection. Citizens who treat others with kindness will be guarded by their friends and neighbors. Their presence in that town, no matter how common, will make a difference, and if they need help, the boys from the bar, the ladies from their churches, the kids from their kids' school, and neighbors from all over town will pitch in.

That's the theory. It usually worked, but Ruth Martin had as many friends as anyone, and none of them did her any good at all.

We mourned her loss, and we mourned what her absence said about our lovely little town.

As I read the daily "Martin Still Missing" story in the *Lincoln Courier*—often on the back page, although it was easily the biggest local story of the day—I remembered the afternoon we spent with Ruth looking at houses.

As she cheerfully drove us from one home to another, she mentioned recently showing a particular house to a single man. I asked her if she ever worried about being alone in an empty house with a stranger.

"No," she laughed. "Not in Lincoln."

• • •

As June turned to July without another word about Mike Mansfield or from Ruth Martin, I found myself worrying less and less about them. "The Wanderer" notes indicated Mike was physically all right and the police still did not consider Smrekar a strong suspect in either disappearance. In spite of everything, I wanted to believe that it was unlikely that both Mike's disappearance and Ruth's were connected to Smrekar.

Slowly the town thought less about Ruth Martin. There were so many unanswered questions. Maybe she ran away with somebody? If she were dead, wouldn't they have found the body by now?

Lincoln jumped into summer as it had for years, with a multitude of softball leagues and the county fair. Some college women, mostly teachers' wives, had asked me to coach their softball team, and so we busied ourselves during the humid, dusty summer with work, softball, and drinking beer after practice.

The women were looking only for a little exercise, but we were thrown into a league filled with nineteen-year-old physical education majors. The results were gruesome, and the beer was especially needed one hot muggy night in August when we lost to a team that hadn't won a game in two summers. As we trudged off the field, I saw our opponents jumping around like World Series winners and heard them making plans for an impromptu victory party.

The next morning, I heard the news. While we were drowning our sorrows and our opponents were celebrating, a twenty-one-year-old housepainter named Michael Drabing broke into the Schneider farmhouse on the outskirts of Lincoln. He stabbed to death the parents, Lloyd and Phyllis Schneider, and one of their three daughters, Terri. Another daughter escaped through a window.

Drabing was arrested later that night when he limped to the emergency room of the Lincoln hospital for treatment of a knife wound he had received while hacking the Schneider family to pieces. He calmly told the doctor how he received the wound, and the doctor called the police.

The town was in an uproar. The Ruth Martin case wasn't settled, and there was always the slim chance she was still alive—that she had left of her own choice. But the Schneider family had no choice, and talk of a lynching was muttered throughout the town.

In the drugstore on the town square, a block away from where Drabing sat unrepentant in the old Lincoln jail, an elderly gentleman I didn't know hobbled up to me and sputtered, "Goddammit, somebody ought to do something about that son of a bitch! We've had enough!" Then he coughed and quietly said it again. "We've had enough."

The police quickly moved Drabing out of the Lincoln jail that couldn't safeguard record albums and a guitar and moved him thirty miles away to a newer facility in Decatur. There wasn't much else for the police to do because Drabing admitted to the murders, claiming he wanted to lead a revolution to overthrow the upper classes. Part of his plan called for him to kill rich people, much like Charles Manson had done.

The Schneider family was not particularly rich, but he later said he killed them for practice. The three had been stabbed a combined total of ninety times.

Softball wasn't much fun after that, but we did have one consolation. There was another Schneider daughter, who played softball on a very bad team, one that hadn't won a game in two summers, who on the night of the murders was out celebrating a long-awaited victory instead of trudging home to her death.

The team the Schneider girl's team defeated was mine. Coaches, of course, hate to lose, but if the loss of our team of adult women looking for a little exercise saved a life… Well, maybe sometimes losing wasn't so bad.

Chapter IX

The town was still in an uproar when the students arrived for the fall semester a few weeks later, blissfully unaware of our murderous summer. Mike's friends had graduated and been replaced with a new crop of wide-eyed, nervous, cocky, hopeful, and frightened freshmen. More than half of last year's students were gone—graduated, flunked out, dropped out, or transferred. Mike, Smrekar, and Patti Davis were a dim memory in the minds of a few sophomores. No one else had heard of them. So the fall of 1976 was a new beginning, and what a beginning it was. Everything clicked. The students had an excellent trio of student senate officers who worked hard to promote a good campus atmosphere.

The chemistry that fall was the best I had ever felt. The students seemed more attuned to what we were doing and why they were there. Everyone seemed closer to one another—students and teachers, blacks and whites, dorm directors and residents. It meant more work for me, and much more satisfaction. Instead of spending time trying to learn who started a dorm fight, I helped student groups, who all seemed to have elected strong leaders, plan and run more campus events than the college had ever seen.

The Friday afternoon prayer meetings became so popular that I might as well have cancelled the Friday night film series on campus. From the president to the janitor, dorm directors and faculty, and lots of students, we were all down at Bachelors III solving the problems of the school and the world and having a hell of a good time in the process.

The year was off to a great start.

• • •

It was a pleasant fall, but an ironic one. Usually the soothing, relaxing times came from the town, as needed tranquilizers for the emotional upheaval on campus. Now the campus was a series of pleasant surprises and small victories while the shocks came from the *Courier*'s reports on Michael Drabing.

Ruth Martin was almost forgotten by the townspeople as they eagerly watched the local judicial system crank up for its biggest trial in years. Ruth was hardly mentioned by anyone as Drabing's grand jury indictment and pre-trial hearings unfolded. The man admitted to the murders again, but his lawyer claimed his client was insane when he killed the Schneider family.

Most of the town assumed Drabing wouldn't be punished enough, and it was in that context that Ruth Martin's name resurfaced. "They should fry that son of a bitch," a construction worker told me at the bar one Friday afternoon. "Killin' four people and all he'll get is free room and board for life."

"Four people? He's only charged with killing three, isn't he?"

"Yeah, I know," he answered, "but he musta killed Ruth Martin, too, and nobody's done a goddamn thing about that."

"But how do you know Drabing killed Martin? I never heard of any connection between Drabing and her?"

"Well, figure it out. How many goofballs can this town have, besides the college kids? It's gotta be him. No one else around here would do somethin' like that, and that's why they really ought to burn that asshole."

He took another slug of his beer and turned away. I went back to my table, wondering if he was right.

Ruth's name came up again a week later. The local police chief was on campus for a panel discussion on the constitutional rights of college students. He arrived at the student union early while I was setting up the chairs, and we talked about the state of the town. I told him about my neighborhood back in Chicago and how different and safe Lincoln felt.

"Yeah," he said sadly, rubbing his hand over his crew-cut. "You know, until this summer, Lincoln averaged only one murder every four and a half years."

"Four and a half years? That means if Ruth Martin is dead, that's uh, eighteen years' worth of murders in one summer."

He grunted and said, "Tell me about it." The fact that Drabing was caught and would be punished seemed no consolation to him at all.

• • •

The Prayer Meeting on Friday afternoon, October 1, was one of the best. We all began saying we'd leave early, in time to eat and see *Easy Rider* on campus that night; however, as the afternoon turned to evening, we realized we were having too much fun to leave for a rerun of a shotgun spattering Peter Fonda over the countryside.

The highlight of the night was watching two Secret Service agents trying to blend into the crowd at the bar. President Gerald Ford was making a campaign stop in

Lincoln in eight days, and apparently these guys were checking out the town for political crazies. Colleagues of theirs had talked to me on campus, asking if there were any political radicals left over from the 60s. I told them as long as Gerald Ford didn't try to bring back Prohibition, he was safe.

The agents at the bar gave new meaning to the word "clash." Patterned coats, striped pants, and checkered shirts apparently made them think they'd pass as locals. As one student asked me, "God! Does Washington think we're that stupid?" Then he laughed and said, "Don't answer that."

Finally one of the students stood up and said, "I'm gonna get me a free drink."

"How're you going to do that?" I asked.

"Watch."

He walked over to the bar and stood next to one of the agents, waiting to get the bartender's attention. Then I heard him say, "Boy, I hear Ford is comin' to town next week. He sure is something, ain't he?"

The agent immediately perked up and began talking to our intrepid but thirsty student. An hour later, the student staggered back to our table; he hadn't spent a dime. As he was telling us about his conversation with the agents, he stopped mid-sentence and said, "Hey, I just thought of something. That's Mr. Hartnett's tax money paying for those drinks!"

The kids all thought that was funny, and so did I.

• • •

I didn't sleep enough Saturday morning, and I wasn't really awake when I scanned the *Courier* over a bowl of cereal. Nonetheless, the headline caught my eye.

I took in the news and thought, "My god, *another* murder; no, two of them. Couple named Jay Fry and his pregnant wife, Robin. Don't know 'em. *Finally*, someone I don't know."

I went back to bed for another hour's sleep. Barbara and I spent most of the day in Bloomington, shopping and seeing a movie. We missed the ten o'clock news and never gave Jay and Robin Fry another thought.

I woke up Sunday morning, looked out the window at the gorgeous autumn morning, and groaned. It was time for the college's special Bicentennial Convocation, with guest speakers who would receive honorary degrees amidst all the traditional pomp and ceremony that a tiny college of five-hundred students can muster.

Our president, J. Richard Stoltz, was the pomp expert on campus. He lived for events like this and always assumed that the rich guy getting the degree would solve the school's financial problems with a big, fat donation. (Clement Stone, the insurance magnate, was granted a degree once and, rather than giving the school a lot of money, responded by giving everyone at the school a copy of his book.)

I hated events like this and felt sorry for myself that beautiful morning. I'd have to give up the Bear's game on TV and wear my dusty cap and gown to hear someone I didn't care about give a boring speech so the president could think he was back at Columbia University where he came from.

Just before noon the phone rang.

"Mike? This is Tom down at the station. Something's come up, and we need to talk to you."

"Okay, shoot."

"No, not on the phone. Could you come down to the station? Now? We don't want to talk over the phone."

"Oh. Well, okay. See ya soon."

Saved! I didn't have to go to the damn convocation. Even if the talk with Tom was only five minutes, I could tell Stoltz the call had come just before I was leaving for campus, and I felt it was too serious to ignore—whatever the hell it was. With any luck, I'd be home in time for the opening kickoff.

As I drove downtown, I thought it strange that Tom was working on a Sunday morning and wouldn't talk over the phone, but I was too pleased to be missing the J. Richard Stoltz Variety Show to give it much thought.

My smug attitude vanished when I walked into the detective's squad room and saw Tom and Bill slumped over their desks, staring into space. They looked exhausted.

"Boy do you guys look terrible," I said brightly. "What the hell are you doing here on Sunday morning?"

"Thanks for coming," Bill answered, ignoring my cheery greeting with a yawn. I'd never seen him look so tired, but when he looked up at me, I knew he was more than tired. Those eyes had seen something and been wounded by the sight. Something more than sleep would be needed to heal them.

"We need you to do something for us, but we couldn't talk about it over the phone."

"Sure, I'll help, but what the hell is so all-fired serious that we can't talk over the phone?"

"We have to keep this absolutely quiet," Tom answered, then he yawned. "We need you to check and see if any of the students saw Smrekar on campus this weekend. But *nobody* can know what you're doing or why you're asking."

"That ought to be easy since I don't know why I'm asking," I told them.

"What do you mean you don't know?" Bill asked irritably.

"I mean I don't know. After all this time, why do you care if Smrekar was on campus this weekend? As far as I know, nobody's seen him around here for months, and what difference would it make anyway?"

"Jesus Christ, Mike," Tom said in amazement. "Didn't you read the paper yesterday?"

"Not really, why?"

"Did you read about Jay Fry getting killed late Friday night, and his wife, too?"

"Just vaguely. What about them?"

"Near as we can figure, they'd been out that night, and when they came home, someone was waiting for them with a shotgun. He shot 'em at point blank range. Blew 'em to pieces."

I didn't want to ask, but I knew I couldn't avoid it. I looked into Tom's shell-shocked eyes for an instant and finally got the words out. "But who is Jay Fry? And what does he have to do with Smrekar?"

"Jay Fry was one of the Kroger employees who chased Smrekar out of the store that night. Jay Fry was supposed to testify against Smrekar next week."

Chapter X

Stunned silence is a cliché used too many times to describe too many situations. But as I stood in the squad room on a cheery Sunday morning while most of our neighbors prayed in church, and I stared into the shell-shocked eyes of an exhausted cop, it's the only phrase that fit.

I don't know how long we looked at each other, but it wasn't long enough and didn't comfort either of us. Finally I had to ask the question, although the answer was obvious.

"That means Ruth and Mike . . ." I couldn't finish it.

"Yeah."

"Jesus Christ. Then it was all true, all this time."

"I guess so."

More silence, then anger. "So what do we do about the fucker?"

"There's a chance he might have stopped on campus to see a friend or somebody before he went to the Fry's. It would help if a student could confirm that he was in town, maybe place him on campus before the murders."

"If anybody saw him, I'll find out. Got a picture I can show people?"

"Somewhere in here," Tom answered and began searching through a stack of papers on his desk. "Here's one," he said, handing it to me. "We took this when we booked him on the shoplifting charge."

There was that face again, almost a year to the day since he walked out of the Judicial Board hearing, promising to drop out of school. The long hair, greasy and straggly, framing the thin mouth that had bragged, "I'll get out of it." And the eyes. I had forgotten how grimy his appearance was, but I remembered the eyes.

"You gotta keep this quiet," Bill warned. "We need witnesses, but they may be afraid to come forward if they know what happened to the other witnesses . . ." His voice trailed off.

"I will," I promised as I tucked the picture in my jacket. I started for the door, then thought of another question. "Have you got a case?"

"Don't ask," Bill answered. He looked at the mess on his desk, then up at the evidence lockers where the burglary evidence was stolen, and he took a deep breath and said it again: "Don't ask."

After I left the station, I climbed into my car and sat there on the empty, Sunday morning town square. I took out the photograph and stared at it.

The questions were finally answered. The burglary in the police station, Mike's disappearance, the letters from the "Wanderer," the blood stains in Ruth's garage—all of it.

This son of a bitch killed four people.

But knowing the answer was no consolation and raised too many more thoughts.

I should never have told Mike to testify.

I should have understood Smrekar better.

I should have fought for his expulsion sooner.

I should not have written those hopeful letters to Mike's mother.

I should have paid more attention to what was going on.

I should have warned Mike after the police burglary, convinced him it was too dangerous to stay involved.

I should have done my job better.

Somehow, I should have known.

• • •

I drove home slowly and walked in the house. Barb was upstairs and shouted down, "What is it this time?"

"Come on down and I'll tell ya. It's really something."

"You always say that, Mike," she joked as she bounced down the stairs and sat next to me in the living room.

After Barbara heard the story and went through her own stunned silence, she finally asked, "What about you?"

"What about me? I'll just try to find someone on campus who saw him."

"No, I mean, what's to keep him from killing you? After saying all those things to him, getting him kicked out of school, giving the evidence to the police." She paused. "Seems like he's killing everybody else."

"Jesus, I never thought of that." And I never had. I was an educator; I worked with kids. I didn't have creeps coming after me with a shotgun.

We sat there without speaking, letting the events of the weekend wash over us like an ice cold shower.

Barbara, who taught psychology at Illinois Central College in the Peoria area, eventually shook her head and said, "No, I take it back. Smrekar won't do anything to you. Or me."

"Why do you think that?"

"Because he's a classic sociopath. He's killing people who stand in his way—people who are a current threat to him. What you did to him was a year ago; it doesn't hurt him *now*. And since it doesn't hurt him now, isn't a threat to him now; he won't act on it. If he killed you, it would be out of revenge, and there's nothing in his behavior pattern to think he murders out of revenge."

"A lousy piece of meat, yes, but not revenge."

• • •

I called President Stoltz later that night and warned him about the bad publicity soon to hit his college. Like all good administrators in the face of a crisis, he said he'd call a meeting.

When I arrived on campus the next morning, a reporter from a Springfield newspaper was waiting for me. I brought him into my office, gave him a chair, offered him coffee, and told him to ask his questions. My father was a newspaper man for most of his life, and I had grown up thinking people should talk to reporters. I was ready and expecting to answer his questions—until the son of a bitch started in on me.

He was Woodward and Bernstein without the tact, without the intelligence, and with only about a fourth of the facts. He thought he was the only smart person in the room, and it was only my appalling ignorance that kept him from convincing me Smrekar was a mass murderer, despite the lack of evidence.

I quickly realized I wasn't going to tell this guy anything, so I just sat at my desk smoking and played dumb.

Mr. News Ace, who looked no more than twenty-five, then changed the topic and began berating me for violating Smrekar's constitutional rights by not allowing a lawyer at his expulsion hearing.

"Wait a minute," I interrupted. "I thought you said he was a mass murderer? What's wrong with trying to get a mass murderer off campus?"

The young reporter smiled condescendingly and said, "Yes, but you didn't know then he was a mass murderer when you violated his rights."

"Oh, well, that explains it."

I was ready to throw him out of my office, but I imagined tomorrow's headline: "College Officials Silent; What Are They Hiding?" and I knew Stoltz would go berserk over that, so I sat there and played stupid again.

Apparently the reporter finally decided I was too dumb to be useful, and he left for a better source.

After he huffed and puffed his way out of my office, I sat at my desk alone and wondered about it all. Despite his arrogance and his conclusion jumping, he did have the basic facts straight: Four people were murdered. And Smrekar had killed them.

• • •

President Stoltz called his meeting later that morning. I reported what I knew and how important the police said secrecy was. He ordered the deans and me to make no statement to the press. He would do all the talking for us.

However, it quickly became clear that the "secret" was already public news. I was eating a sandwich at the Gem Lunch with a friend when I heard someone telling others that "one of the college kids" had killed the Fry couple and Ruth Martin because they were supposed to testify against him.

I turned to see who it was, but I didn't recognize him. He looked like a farmer, wearing overalls and a seed company cap—and was flushed with the excitement of knowing something important. The small-town communication system was in high gear.

The Gem's customers stopped eating and listened to the farmer tell the story that he claimed came from "someone who knows."

I noticed people's reactions were different from the other murders. They were angry when they heard of the Drabing murders, but not now. This time people were afraid. If someone would kill three people over a piece of meat, what else might he do? Whom else might he kill?

● ● ●

The story was out. Townspeople knew what had happened—or thought they knew. By the time I had returned from lunch, the story had spread through the faculty, and the phone calls started.

"Mike? I just heard about Smrekar. Did he really kill all those people?"

"The police are looking into it, but I don't know for sure who did what."

"I had Smrekar in a class last year and flunked him. Should I be worried? Is he going to come after me, too?"

"No, no, no. If Smrekar killed those people, then what's he doing is getting rid of people who are a threat to him now. He's not killing them out of revenge, so you should be safe."

I said all that, hoping Barbara was right.

The next call came from the meekest, most mild-mannered faculty member on campus. "I, uh, just wanted you to know that I've heard the Smrekar stories going around campus. Don't you think you're in danger, Mike?"

"Me? Well, no, not really. What I did to him happened

a year ago. He's got too much to worry about now without bothering to settle an old score."

"I hope you're right, but I wanted you to know that you're welcome to borrow my sawed-off shotgun if you want."

"YOU'VE got a sawed-off shotgun?"

"You bet I do. A man's got to protect his family."

"Well, um, thanks for the offer, but I don't know how to use one of those things. I'd probably blow my own foot off with it."

"Oh no you wouldn't. It's not that hard to use."

"No, I don't think so. I'm not in any real danger, but thanks anyway."

"Okay, but if you change your mind, just let me know."

"I'll do that."

The rest of the afternoon was spent talking quietly to students and showing them the picture of Russell Smrekar that I had stared at so often within the past twenty-four hours. No one had seen him. In fact, none of the students had heard about the murders, and for once I was happy that the students and the townspeople did not mingle very much.

But the phone calls from the faculty and friends continued. Everyone tried to be helpful, but by the time I drove home, I was frightened again.

Barbara and I spent much of the evening trying to rebuild each other's confidence, but it was like cupping water in our hands. We'd have it for a while, clear and bright, then another phone call from a helpful friend would come, and the water would slip through our fingers.

If we weren't in any danger, why was everyone so afraid for us?

Chapter XI

The next morning at the Gem, I heard about the plot to kill Gerald Ford. "Can't you see the connection, Jake?" asked a fellow sitting in the next booth. "Lincoln was killed in the Ford Theater, and when he comes to town Saturday, Ford's supposed to stop and eat lunch at the Lincoln Hotel. That's where he'll be shot."

"That's crazy," his friend answered. "Sure there was a note on the bodies sayin' there'd be more killin's, but it didn't say nothin' 'bout murderin' no president. That's just rumor."

A note?

I interrupted them and asked about it. They both swore the police had found a note tossed casually on what was left of the Frys. In the scrap of paper, the killer bragged that more people would die.

So much for a hearty breakfast.

When I got to my office, I called Tom and asked him about it.

"Has that shit spread to the campus, too?" he growled. "There was no damn note and no, Ford ain't gonna be shot in Lincoln."

And Tom had more good news. He did not elaborate, but said the police were slowly building a case against Smrekar. There wasn't enough evidence to arrest him yet, but they were getting closer.

"Are you just sayin' that to make me feel better?" I asked.

"Hey," Tom answered. "It makes us all feel better."

• • •

Soon after I had hung up the phone, it rang again. I picked it up, said hello, and waited.

No answer.

"Come on, come on," I said. "I'm in a hurry."

Still no voice. Then strange, electronic-sounding noises, like a dying computer, began in the distance and became louder.

I don't know how long I sat there listening to the inhuman groaning and creaking. It felt like time had stopped, and I was suspended, glued to the phone like a man standing all alone and cold on railroad tracks, mesmerized by the shriek of the oncoming whistle.

As I listened and felt the knot in my stomach grow larger, Harold, a sophomore, burst into my office.

"Oh, god, Mr. Hartnett, I've got to talk to you right away! This time it's too much!" Harold was out of breath, as if he had just run from his dorm room.

I snapped out of what was by then almost a hypnotic trance and hung up. "Uh, sit down, Harold. Lemme get a cup of coffee first from next door," I mumbled, needing a minute or two to change gears.

"Well, okay, but this is important," Harold sputtered while running a hand through his unkempt hair and fidgeting in the chair as soon as he sat in it.

I went into the campus mailroom, poured a cup of coffee, and tried to calm down. When I returned I said, "Incidentally, I was on the phone when you burst in and interrupted me. Couldn't you have waited until I got off?

You don't know who I was talking to. For all you know, it was real important." (For all I knew, it was.)

"I'm sorry, Mr. Hartnett, but this just couldn't wait."

This was probably the semester's 212th crisis for Harold. Harold was a nice kid, but he wasn't smart, he wasn't good looking, he wasn't handsome, he wasn't funny, he wasn't mature, he was just . . . Harold.

"Now Harold, I'm real busy. All kinds of serious stuff is going on around here, and I just don't have time for anything minor, believe me. Are you sure this is serious? You know we talked before about your handling things yourself?"

"Absolutely, Mr. Hartnett. But I'm really at the breaking point this time."

"Okay, Harold, what is it?"

"You remember the last time I was in here, 'cause my roommate wouldn't always remember to lock our door when he left the room?"

"Yes, Harold."

"Well, he did it again."

"Did what again?"

"Forgot to lock the door."

"And"

"That's it."

"Was your room robbed? Or vandalized?"

"Nope."

"Just unlocked?"

"Yup. What are you going to do about it, Mr. Hartnett?"

I stared at good old Harold until I realized he was serious. Then all sorts of answers sprang to mind, things like, "Have you thought about dropping out of school?"; "There's always suicide"; and ultimately, "Why me, Lord?".

I think Harold must have read my mind, though, because he finally said, "On second thought, maybe I better come back later."

"Helluva idea, Harold. Helluva idea."

• • •

At least Harold took my mind off the phone call. After Harold stumbled out of the office, I decided it must be something wrong with the phone company and forgot about it.

I spent the rest of the day showing Smrekar's picture to students. No one recognized him or knew why I was asking.

Once again I was thankful that the students didn't read the local paper or listen to our town's radio station. None of them were aware of the murders or the rumors. Most didn't even know President Gerald Ford was coming to town in four days.

But the faculty had heard all the rumors, and they were concerned for themselves and me. I received offers for two pistols and a "killer" guard dog that day. It was nice to know so many people cared; it also scared the hell out of me.

"I gotta stop listening to this shit," I mumbled to myself on the way home that evening. "Barbara is right about Smrekar. Everything is fine."

I arrived home and was greeted at the door by the vice president of the college, Dale Brummet.

"I was thinking about you and Barb while on my way home," he said after holding the door open for me, "so I decided to drop in for a minute and talk. I wanted you to know there are rumors going around; I suppose you've heard them, about Smrekar coming after you?"

"Oh, yeah, we've heard them," I answered, then gave what had become my standard speech about how Smrekar wasn't killing for revenge, and we were safe.

"Well, if you do think there's anything to it, don't hang around here. We can handle your job for a while if you want to get out."

"Thanks, Dale, but I think we're okay. Maybe this weekend we'll get away for a couple days, not because of the danger, but just to get away." I couldn't tell the well-meaning vice president that if we did leave town for the weekend it would be to get away from helpful friends like him.

• • •

That night Barbara and I talked a long time about our friends' offers to loan us guns. We were in favor of gun control and didn't think anyone should have guns in their home. Now that theory was being tested by a very ugly reality, and it was time to put up or shut up. Did we really believe what we had said so glibly all these years?

We knew the liberal arguments. We knew about the accidents in the home, the increased danger of being shot by a burglar if the victim has a gun, the knowledge that a television set and some silver weren't worth taking a life.

But now we weren't talking about a petty burglar. There was a cretin out there who had proved to the world that he could look someone in the eye and pull the trigger as easily as stepping on a bug. And if the wife happened to be there, well, he no doubt had extra shells for his shot-gun.

Barbara and I had used words and reason all our lives to succeed in school, acquire and keep jobs, and create comfortable lives for ourselves. A student had once told me that her family was rich because they had more than they needed. We were rich in the same way, and we had achieved that status through honest hard work and our ability to reason logically with the world.

But we knew Smrekar wouldn't give us a chance to say a word. He wouldn't care that we were nice people, that we didn't deserve to die. He'd see it as just stepping on another couple of bugs.

If Smrekar intended to kill me, my only chance would be to shoot him first.

But the police had told me Jay Fry had guns in his home, and they were of no more use to him than a borrowed pistol probably would be to us.

Finally the whole episode just made me mad. I wasn't going to change the way I lived or what I believed in because of a spineless little creep like Smrekar. If the only way I could continue my job was to carry a damn gun, then it was time for a new job.

Barbara agreed, and after we had decided to say no to the gun offers, the anger left me. I didn't even feel proud that I had stuck to my principles. I just hoped I was right. To be on the safe side, though, we decided it would be a good idea to go away for the weekend.

• • •

We said no to the guard dog, too. We had no place to keep a large dog and besides, he'd probably eat our dog, Sam, a beagle/basset mutt, and our three cats.

Not that they were any protection. Sam would let anyone in the house in exchange for a pat on the head. The cats wouldn't lower themselves to pay attention to an intruder unless they thought he was afraid of them. Then they'd want to sit in his lap and stare into his nervous eyes. For that matter, the cats thought we were intruders.

As I walked Sam that night, I lectured him about how he could be a little meaner, but he was too busy watering the stately oak trees on our block to listen.

As we walked along Eighth Street, past the darkened school and the quiet hospital, a car turned the corner and drove slowly towards us, its headlights especially bright on the dark, tree-shrouded street.

Immediately I jumped behind the nearest tree, pulling Sam with me. The car passed us slowly and, as I stepped back onto the sidewalk, I realized how automatically I had reacted to the car's headlights and began to laugh.

When I was a little boy, about ten years old, I lived on the south side of Chicago. The neighborhood had grown increasingly dangerous, and white and black gangs sprung up like weeds. My friends and I learned very quickly to run or hide from any slowly cruising cars at night and now, twenty-some years later, in a town that averaged one murder every four-and-a-half years, I had come full circle.

I laughed again, and Sam looked up at me as if to say, "We can't stand here all night. I've got business."

Chapter XII

On Wednesday morning the phone was ringing as I ran into my office, tossing my coat on a chair. It was the same as the first call—strange electronic noises— eerie, and maddening.

I looked at my watch and then sat there listening in vain for human breathing or a familiar background noise.

After three minutes I said, "Hey, asshole, if I'm supposed to be getting a message from this, it's not coming through. Am I supposed to be afraid, or what?"

After another three minutes I said quietly, "You chicken-shit son of a bitch" and hung up.

I quickly called the switchboard operator who told me the call came from off campus. She did not recognize the voice which asked for me by name. But she knew the caller was male.

So what the hell was going on? Smrekar wasn't the type to make threats or give warnings. Why was I getting these calls now? Being in charge of campus discipline made me a few enemies each year; maybe it was just a coincidence? The Judicial Board had expelled a student from the dorms for possession of marijuana the week before, and though he complained bitterly enough at the time, he hardly seemed imaginative enough for a scheme like this.

There were no answers, but there was a solution. I walked over to the gymnasium and borrowed a referee's whistle from Al Pickering, the men's basketball coach. The next time the son of a bitch called, I was going to shatter his eardrum, then go to the hospital emergency room and see who walked in holding his head.

But until I had solved this little mystery, I was not going to tell Barbara. She was worried enough about the bigger, more dangerous mystery.

• • •

I called the police when I returned to my office with my whistle. Tom was concerned when I told him about the phone calls and said if they continued, he'd try to have my phone tapped.

He told me the police had a phone mystery of their own. Recently someone had called the station late at night and set off a noise loud enough to damage the eardrum of the policewoman who had taken the call.

He also told me more about the case. Jay and Robin had gone out drinking that evening and returned home about 1:00 AM. The police thought Smrekar was in the house by then, waiting for them. They thought Jay died first, probably lunging for a rifle he kept in the house to protect his wife and their unborn baby. Tom said Jay's head was virtually blown to pieces. Then Smrekar calmly turned his smoking shotgun towards Robin and killed her. I don't know how far along Robin was in her pregnancy, but the life growing in her belly was gone too.

Jay's sister, who lived next door, heard the shotgun blasts, looked out her window, and saw a man leaving the house. She went to investigate. By the time she arrived and discovered the bits and pieces of her brother and his pregnant wife scattered around the floor and sticking to the walls like wet confetti, Smrekar was gone.

Later, after the police had finished their investigation of the crime scene and the bodies had been taken away, Tom got a phone call from the medical examiner. It seems the police had missed part of Jay's brain. The police returned to the little house with the makeshift bait shop in the back and looked again. They found the rest of Jay's brain in a house plant.

Tom pleaded with me not to tell anyone what I knew. I promised him I wouldn't and hung up.

I knew I'd keep my word and not talk about it. I didn't even want to think about it.

• • •

Barbara called me later that morning. She had no classes that day except for an evening extension class in Morton, a Peoria suburb fifty miles away. Sitting at home alone that day had given her too much time to think, and she sounded nervous and out of sorts.

I told her to come to campus before she left for class, and we could have a cup of coffee together and talk about our plans for our weekend getaway.

When she arrived, we walked over to the student union and stood at the coffee machine while I groped in my pocket for change. I finally grabbed everything in my pocket and pulled it out. There in my hand, amidst the dimes and pennies, laid the whistle.

Barb asked me what it was for and without thinking I said, "Oh, in case I get another phone call." The instant I said it, I realized my mistake.

"WHAT phone call?"

Of all the things I am not good at, lying to Barbara is probably at the top of the list. I knew I would frighten her more if she thought I was covering up something, so I told her the truth.

As Barbara stood there listening to me, I could see the strain of the last few days begin to show. And these phone calls were the last straw. Tears formed in her eyes, and my wonderful pillar of logical, rational strength melted away.

I held her tightly while she sobbed, "Why us?" but I had no answer. We stood there a moment, trying to hug away the fear.

Then two African American sophomore girls who often joined us at Prayer Meetings entered the union and saw us hugging. "Isn't that cute," one of them teased. "Old folks, and they're still in love."

They didn't realize Barbara was crying. While still holding her, I shook my head and waved the girls away.

Barbara was fine in a few minutes; she was too strong a person not to be. But when I made my usual offer to drive her to her night class, for the first time she said yes. Usually she would say no, not wanting me to waste my evening driving a hundred miles to sit in a library for three hours. This time she said yes.

● ● ●

After returning from Morton that night, I walked Sam and thought about Robin Fry.

In her early twenties, pregnant, and excited about the future—Robin and her husband return home and find Russ Smrekar waiting in their darkened living room. Robin is startled when she turns on the light and sees this strange man standing in her home holding a shotgun.

She doesn't recognize him because she has never seen him before and wonders why this creepy-looking character is standing there with a smirk on his face and a gun in his hand. As Robin turns to her young husband to ask

"Who is this guy?" he recognizes the intruder, shouts something, and brushes past her trying to reach his own gun.

Before she can say the words, Smrekar pulls the trigger at point-blank range. She sees her husband's head explode into bits and pieces and splatter across the modest, well-kept living room. She does not see the look in the intruder's eyes when he killed her husband.

What are Robin's thoughts as she and Smrekar turn away from the gristle and blood on the floor and look at each other? Is she in shock, not realizing she is next? Does she fear for her unborn baby? Herself? Does she scream for her sister-in-law next door? Is there time to hate before Smrekar pulls the trigger again? Probably not, and certainly no time afterwards, because death is immediate and bloody and final.

And what of Smrekar's thoughts as he turns away from his first victim and looks at Robin and points the gun at her? If she says anything to him, does it make any difference at all? Do her words make him pause for even an instant? Is he afraid? Does it occur to him that maybe Robin will be frightened into silence, and he doesn't have to kill her? Does it ever occur to him that a shoplifting conviction isn't worth all this? Does he notice that she's pregnant? After he is finished, does he feel any guilt at all as he leaves the house?

I doubt it.

I was thinking more about Robin's last moments than those of Ruth Martin or Mike Mansfield because I knew more details about the end of Robin's life, and because I knew she must have looked into Smrekar's eyes, as I did that sunny afternoon in his dorm room, and seen the same emptiness.

Then another car turned the corner and drove slowly towards me, its headlights bringing me back to the present. I jumped behind a tree, pulling Sam with me.

Chapter XIII

Thursday was more of the same—fruitless conversations, foolish rumors, and fear. The police were still trying to stop the rumors, find more evidence, prepare for Ford's visit, and live with the memory of the Frys lying dead in their living room.

Tom said Smrekar was scheduled to appear in court the following Monday for his shoplifting trial. The police didn't expect him to show up, but they had set Monday as a private deadline for gathering evidence against him. *If* they had enough evidence, and *if* he appeared, it would be much easier to arrest him in a Lincoln courtroom than it would be to hunt him down in Joliet.

I told the police to expect Smrekar to walk into the courtroom on Monday morning acting as if nothing had happened. He would arrive confident that the charges would be dismissed, as they had been in the dorm burglary. After all, two of the three eyewitnesses were gone. Surely the judge would decide that poor Mr. Smrekar had suffered enough with this cloud hanging over his head and would dismiss the charge.

If the judge only postponed the trial, well, then there would be time to eliminate the final witness.

He'll show up perfectly content, with his version of an innocent smile on his face, and Patti lapping at his heels like a puppy.

That thought just added to the already large knot in my stomach, and I was grouchier and more distracted than usual.

The two African American girls who had teased Barbara and me in the student union the day before came to see me that morning. "You folks all right?" Andreta asked.

"To tell you the truth, Andreta, I don't know."

"Well," Eloise said, "you got a fine lady there. Don't you be causing her to cry like that."

"I'm trying. Believe me, I'm trying."

• • •

That night, all hell broke loose. The rumors, each a bizarre ingredient in a nightmarish recipe, finally filtered through to the campus and were blended together with overactive teenage imaginations.

The first call came shortly after dinner while Barbara and I were planning our getaway weekend. It was Pat, one of the women's dorm directors. "Well, boss, the rumors are here, tra la, tra, la. To hear these ladies talk, you'd think they're all being murdered in their beds tonight."

"What are they hearing?"

"Oh, hell, I don't know if I even remember 'em all. Let's see, there's the one about the note on the bodies sayin' there'd be more killings. Another that says you and the J Board are going to get your fannies shot off for throwing that guy out of the dorms and confiscatin' his pot. Of course there's the one about the commies gonna kill Ford on Saturday, but they killed the Frys first and then a few students later to cover their tracks. I think that about covers it."

"Anything I can do?"

"Nah. I'm gonna have a dorm meeting and try to settle 'em down, but I don't think it'll help much. Just wanted to warn ya to be ready for a few calls tonight."

They started about an hour later and lasted till midnight. Call #1: "My god, Mr. Hartnett, you've got to get out! You're going to be murdered!"

"Who is this? Kathy? Listen sweetie, I've heard all the stories, and there's nothing to be afraid of. Nobody's going to kill anybody."

"But the note on the bodies said . . ."

"I already talked to the police about it. There really, *honestly,* was no note."

"But everyone involved is gonna be killed."

"Nope. Honest, Kathy, it won't happen."

"But don't you think you at least ought to get out of town for a while, just in case?"

"No, Kathy, I don't. None of the students need to leave, either."

"I don't know, Mr. Hartnett. I know I'm going home early for the weekend. You ought to, too."

"Kathy, I am home."

Call #2: "Mr. Hartnett? This is Lisa. I want to know what you're gonna do about protecting my boyfriend."

"Tom Hammerton? What does Tom need protecting for?"

"Don't give me that, Mr. Hartnett. You know damn well he was on the J Board when they kicked Smrekar out of the dorms. Now somebody's gonna kill him, and this goddamn school better protect him. For all the money we pay around here, this school's got an obligation to do something about it!"

"Lisa, it won't happen. Believe me, Tom is safe."

"Oh yeah? What if you're wrong? You gonna tell me at his funeral that you made a mistake?"

Call #3: "Hey, Mike, this is Andreta. I know why Barb was cryin' the other day in the union. I'm sorry we were teasin' ya. You all gettin' out of town?"

The other calls were more of the same, and to every worried and frightened student, I offered logic, reason, empathy, and truth. None of it worked. The only argument that had any effect was my saying that I wasn't leaving town. That seemed the only way to alleviate the fears.

After the last phone call, we went to bed and hugged each other quietly as we had done every night since we learned about the Frys.

Finally Barbara smiled and said, "After all this, we can't go away this weekend now, can we?"

"No, I guess we can't," I said, and hugged her again.

• • •

I went to school early the next morning and discovered the campus was half empty. The students had left town in wholesale numbers, taking the early train to Chicago that usually stopped for one or two townspeople. (I wondered what the conductor thought when he saw more than a hundred teenagers waiting nervously at dawn to get out of this sleepy little town.)

Then the phone calls from the parents began. The students were back home and had breathlessly shared the rumors with their bewildered parents. I spent the afternoon trying to calm down the parents, and I explained the same kinds of things to them that I had said to their children the night before.

It didn't work. Their kids were so convincing, and after all, what college administrator is going to admit his school can't protect its students?

Finally I had an idea: an argument that seemed to satisfy the parents.

"Tell you what. I'll prove to you the campus is safe. Gerald Ford is supposed to speak here tomorrow. He's on a train going through small towns in Illinois, and he's going to give a speech here and then eat lunch before going on. If you don't believe me now, fine. But watch your evening news tomorrow and see if Ford does stop in Lincoln. After all the assassinations and attempts, the Secret Service certainly wouldn't let him stop here if they thought there was the slightest chance of danger. If the town is safe enough for the President of the United States, then it's probably safe enough for your daughter."

That argument seemed to work, so I used it again and again on the other hysterical calls that came in that afternoon. But as I hung up from the last call around 4:30 and prepared to get out of the office before the next call came through, I realized the flaw in the argument. What if there's a crisis and Ford has to cancel? What if he gets sick and can't speak?

The parents would never believe it. If something did happen and Ford cancelled his stop in Lincoln, those parents might *never* send their kids back. I may have wiped out half of the college's enrollment. President Stoltz was really going to love me for this one.

• • •

There was nothing I could do about Gerald Ford, so I stopped worrying about it and went downtown to the bar for the Friday prayer meeting. There weren't as many students as usual, but Barbara had returned from her school and about ten of us sat around and talked and drank away the early evening.

The students wanted to know what was going on. Those that remained had taken my word about the danger, but they wondered what had caused the rumors in the first place.

By this time I thought the whole truth would be more helpful than letting the students jump to conclusions. These kids were the leaders of the school—leaders who could influence the other dorm residents not to believe everything they heard. Besides, I was sick of keeping it all to myself.

So I told them, compressing two years of crimes, mysteries, blind leads, assurances, and hopes. Now that I had the answers to their major questions and told the story as if the answers were obvious, the whole thing sounded so simple.

I thought finally telling the whole story might make me feel better. It didn't.

When I finished, I walked to the bar for another Black Russian. Sitting there in another ugly outfit was the Secret Service agent who had bought so many drinks the week before.

"My god," I thought, "was that only a week ago?"

I thought about getting drunk, so I could forget it all for a while. I did drink, but when Barbara and I went home about 7:30, walked Sam, and went to bed, I was still sober.

Chapter XIV

President Gerald Ford came to town on Saturday and, God bless him, made a fool of himself. Lincoln was probably his fourth or fifth stop that day on his train tour, but like a mediocre comedian doing a trite parody of the Leader of the Free World, he announced to the waiting crowd, "I'm really pleased to be here in Joliet today."

As the audience groaned, I turned to Barbara and asked, "When do the bad jokes stop?"

• • •

On Monday Russell Smrekar arrived in court with Patti for his shoplifting trial; he was arrested and charged with murder. The police had found their evidence.

I wasn't happy when I heard the news, and I wasn't relieved. All I could think was, "But do they have a case?"

I waited until the following day to call Tom and ask him. For the first time since the Fry murders, I heard some pride in his voice. "Goddamn right we've got a case."

There was a witness, after all. Jay Fry's sister lived next door and, hearing a loud blast, had looked out her window and saw a skinny white male running out of her brother's home. She ran next door and discovered the bodies of her brother and sister-in-law. She did not identify him at first, but later, after undergoing hypnosis, she identified Smrekar as the man she saw running from the home.

And the police had a speeding ticket issued to Smrekar. He was cited by a state trooper for traveling ninety miles per hour up Interstate 55, the highway separating Lincoln and Joliet. Smrekar was traveling north, away from Lincoln, and the time and speed meant he could have been in Lincoln at the time of the murders.

And finally, there was the twin brother. I don't know if it happened or not, but it was one of the rumors that surfaced after the arrest. Jay Fry had an identical twin, and to see what effect he would have on Smrekar, the police had the accused killer sit in a particular chair facing the door in the detectives' squad room—the same room where Smrekar had stolen the burglary evidence a year earlier. There was a window in the door separating the squad room from the hallway, and the police had Jay's brother stand in front of the window and stare at him.

According to the rumor, Smrekar reacted as if he had seen a ghost.

● ● ●

The next day Kathy, who had suggested the previous Thursday that I should go away for the weekend, came into my office. She said her parents had watched the Saturday night news as I had suggested and saw Gerald Ford make his mistake. As I had hoped, his presence in Lincoln, silly as it turned out to be, convinced them that she should return to school.

I said now that Smrekar had been arrested, her parents could be doubly assured nothing more would happen.

"What's this guy look like, anyway?" Kathy asked.

"Didn't I ever show you his picture? I thought everyone had seen it last week," I said, fishing through the papers on my desk. I finally found his picture and showed it to her.

"Why were you showing this around?"

"The police had asked me to see if any of the students had seen Smrekar on campus the night before the murders."

"Which would have been when?" Kathy asked, straightening up in her chair and nervously fingering her hair.

"Well, let's see. That would have been a week ago Friday night."

"You're kidding."

"No, why?"

She looked at the photograph again and then looked up at me. "Because I think I saw him on campus that day."

It was my turn to say, "You're kidding." I quickly called the police, and they told me to bring her down to the station. I did, and after I brought her to the squad room and introduced her to Tom and Bill, Tom said, "Instead of going through a full-fledged lineup, why don't you look at these six photographs and see if you can pick him out."

He then laid out six black and white photographs on his desk and Kathy huddled over them. She seemed to be having trouble choosing one, so I glanced over her shoulder and studied the six young faces.

Smrekar wasn't there.

Finally Kathy picked up one and said, "I think he's the one, but I don't know if I could swear he was the one I saw on campus that day."

"Ok, thanks," Bill answered. "We'll call you if we need you."

I asked Kathy, who obviously hadn't seen Smrekar on campus, to wait outside the squad room for a moment. When I was alone with the detectives, I kidded them, saying "So you guys are pullin' a fast one now, huh?"

"What do you mean?" Tom asked.

"Smrekar's picture wasn't among the six. You guys threw a phony lineup at her."

Tom shook his head and smiled. "No, we didn't, Mike."

"But Smrekar's picture wasn't there."

"Yes it was," Bill answered.

"Show me."

Once again Bill laid out the six photographs. I looked again. None of them had long hair; most didn't even have a moustache. But just as I was about to repeat my charge, I saw those eyes staring up at me from a clean-cut face.

"Son of a bitch; it is him."

"'Fraid so, friend."

"When did he cut his hair?"

"I dunno, but that's what he looks like now."

"Jesus Christ," I said, suddenly feeling very cold. "Do you realize he could have come to my house looking like that and I wouldn't have recognized him?"

"Well, it's a good thing he didn't, then."

"That's not much goddamn consolation."

• • •

The immediate reaction in town was the same as it was when Michael Drabing was arrested for murdering the Schneider family. "Kill him."

The police were concerned—professionally, that is. To a man, the police did not think Smrekar would be punished enough by the judicial system they had sworn to uphold. But they knew it wasn't their job to punish—just catch and hold safe, so they transferred Smrekar from Lincoln's creaky old lockup to a more substantial jail in Decatur, thirty miles away from where Drabing had been held.

A policeman told me that the Fry relatives were violently upset about the murders, and he was positive that if Smrekar somehow escaped, he wouldn't live more than twenty-four hours. The look on his face and the tone of his voice made me realize he wished it would happen that way. Save the taxpayers some money and give the family—and most everyone in Lincoln—more satisfaction than they were going to get.

Although the rumors persisted and the murders were the main topic of conversation, the town slowly returned to normal. So did the campus, and the Friday prayer meeting was a better-attended, happier event than the week before.

Now, finally, our students could get on with the business of learning, bickering with roommates, falling in love, smoking marijuana, and complaining about the food. And the rest of us could return to teaching, trying to catch kids smoking marijuana, and complaining about the administration.

We were a nice, quiet little college again. Basketball would be starting soon, and the campus began gearing up for Homecoming weekend.

I jumped back to my normal routine with a relish. Harold came back to my office complaining about his roommate again, and I thought it was wonderful to have nothing more serious to worry about than the simple growing pains of a nice group of kids.

The following Wednesday afternoon, I was sitting alone looking over the schedule for next month's homecoming weekend when I heard a familiar voice.

"Hello Mr. Hartnett."

I looked up from a student council proposal for a homecoming bonfire and there she was, grinning at me like a malevolent Cheshire cat, standing there smug and proud and defiant.

It was Patti Davis.

Chapter XV

"Gee, Patti, what a surprise." (Holy shit, what is she doing here?)

"I'll bet it is," she smirked. "Wednesdays are visiting days at the Decatur jail, and since I'm on my way through town, I thought I'd drop in. For a little chat."

(Oh great, a little chat with Patti Davis.) "Well, why don't you sit down."

"I thought you'd never ask."

"So what are you doing these days?" (Why the hell am I talking to her, anyway?)

"Not much, but I'm doin' fine. So's Russ, you know"

(Why does she keep grinning like that?) "Russ is doing fine? How can anybody be fine in jail on murder charges?"

"Because he's going to get off. They don't have any evidence against him, you know. It's all bullshit."

"You really believe that, do you, Patti?"

"Of course I do. Russ didn't do anything, and besides, nobody can prove that he did."

"I don't know, Patti. The police haven't told me a whole lot, but I get the impression they have a real, real good case against him." (I hope.)

"They're all lying. Just like you lied about him robbing the dorms. Everybody lies just to get Russ because they don't like him."

"Then how did the guitar end up in his other girl-friend's house?"

Silence.

"So what're you doing for him?"

"I'm gonna visit him every chance I get; then when he gets out, we're going to go off together."

"Into the sunset, huh?" (With a guy who murdered four people.)

"Yeah, Mike. Into the goddamn sunset."

She stared at me for a moment, then stood up. "I gotta go and see Russ. But I'll be back."

"So I'll see you later, then."

"You bet you will," and she left.

If she'd intended to unnerve me, she'd succeeded. She had smiled that smile at me the entire time she was in my office. And calling me Mike had irritated me most of all. Most of the students, particularly the sophomores, called me Mike, and I liked it. It was informal and cut down one of the artificial barriers between us. But Patti calling me Mike with that mocking, stupid tone of hers was like listening to fingernails on a blackboard.

After I calmed down, I called the police. "Guess who just left my office after a lovely little chat."

"Lemme see," Tom replied. "Farrah Fawcett-Majors?"

"Nope. Patti Davis."

"She did? What did she want?" Tom was all business now.

"Beats the hell out of me. She just came in, told me she was on her way to visit Smrekar, and said he was going to get off."

"Is that right?"

"Tom? Now no kidding around. You do have a good case, don't you?"

"Mike, he's not going to get off. She's gonna have a long wait for her lover boy."

"She better. Geez, it was bad enough to see her and, to top it off, she said she'd come back and visit me again. Just what I need."

"Well, you be sure and let her. And when she does come back, talk to her as long as she wants."

"What the hell for? I don't want to see that bitch ever again, let alone talk to her."

"You never know. She might spill something that would help us with our case. She's probably gonna try to give Smrekar some bullshit alibi, and maybe she'll say something to you that will blow her story. She ain't too bright, you know."

"Oh Tom, goddamnit. Don't do this to me."

"Come on now. You've gone this far with us; you might as well see it through."

"I thought I was done playing junior detective."

"Not quite yet, my friend."

• • •

Getting prepared for homecoming weekend was an enormously complicated and tiring process. I tried to make Lincoln's Homecoming a weekend that was as busy, as exciting, and as classy as those at the large universities who had refused to admit our students. I didn't have the budget to organize any of the glamour events like rock concerts that were common at many schools, but this would be one weekend Lincoln College would not go second-class.

Every organization wanted to sponsor an event surrounding the weekend's focal points—the dance and the opening game of the basketball season. The month following Patti's first visit was filled with a seemingly endless round of meetings, and the workdays stretched into nights and spilled over into the weekends.

I started keeping my Wednesday afternoons open when I realized Patti often visited during that time. If a student came in to see me, I would lie and tell him that I was on my way out, and he should come back the next day.

Patti usually arrived around 1:00 and stayed for a half hour or so. The grin suggesting "I know something you don't" was always the same, and so was the conversation. She was visiting me for the same reason I was talking to her; we were delicately pumping each other for information. When she would finally leave, I always felt as though I'd been in a fencing match. Then I'd call Tom and report another failure.

I don't remember the specifics of each conversation because they were so similar, but certain fragments do remain.

Once when we talked again about her and Smrekar going off together, I interrupted her and said, "Wait a minute. Didn't Russ have a girlfriend back in Joliet? Whatever happened to her?"

"Oh, she's still around."

"Does she visit him like you do?"

"No. She doesn't love him like I do."

(Here goes nothing.) "Patti, are you sure you really love him? Are you sure you aren't caught up in some sort of romantic, 'stand by your man' bullshit?"

Finally she stopped smiling. "I love him. And I'm gonna take care of him, too. I gotta go." She stood up, walked to the door, paused, turned around, and said, "See you next week, Mike."

When Tom heard this, he laughed and said, "Aw, isn't that sweet? Hey, Hartnett, I just thought of a great idea. Maybe you could give away the bride?"

During another little chat, Patti told me of Smrekar's plans to return to Lincoln College.

"He's gonna what?"

"That's right. He's gonna come back here. When he gets out, he's going to come back here and get his tuition money back. You kicked him outta school, and you didn't have any right to."

(I need a cigarette.) "But the Judicial Board found him guilty of the dorm robbery."

"Yeah, but the courts never did. They dropped the charges. And how can you kick him out of school and keep his money if the police didn't find him guilty? See Mike?" The grin was getting wider by the second.

"Well, if he showed up in the business office, the clerks in there would be so scared that they'd give him his money just to get him the hell away."

"Yeah. Lotta people would be scared of him."

I couldn't take the grin or the conversation any longer, and I made up an excuse about a meeting starting in a few minutes.

"Gee, that's too bad, Mike. Our talks are so much fun."

She didn't visit every week, but she continued to make the long drive from Chicago on most Wednesdays. She was more loyal to her lover than I ever thought she would be. On the weeks I did not see her, I would spend the long afternoon alone in my office, shuffling papers and waiting.

For all our smiles and probing conversations, I don't think we learned anything, except, perhaps, the depth of our dislike for each other.

Chapter XVI

The situation changed when the assistant state's attorney for Logan County, John Foltz, subpoenaed me to testify at the grand jury hearing on the Fry murders.

A week before the hearing began, I went down to the courthouse on the town square and met him. He was a handsome, affable young lawyer—recently graduated, I assumed, because the county could never afford any other kind.

He was excited about the biggest case of his career—and nervous, because if he lost, he knew the town would never forgive him for it.

He described how the grand jury operated, and I told him what I knew about Smrekar. Then he asked me about Patti Davis. He said he expected that she would also be testifying, trying to give Smrekar some sort of alibi. What could I tell him about her?

I gave him the facts of her stay at Lincoln College—her involvement with Smrekar and her weekly visits.

When I finished, I inquired, "This isn't directly relevant to the murders, but there was an incident in the dorms during Patti's freshman year that I think really says something about Patti's character. You interested in my telling it to the grand jury?"

I told him the story of Patti and the fishbowl. He grinned and said, "By all means tell it."

• • •

The grand jury hearing was held the following week on a cold, wintery Lincoln morning. I dressed up in my best suit and went down to the old courthouse and waited my turn to talk once again about Russell Smrekar.

The hearing was held on the second floor and since there was no waiting room, and I was too nervous to sit down anyway, I stood in the foyer and looked down over the rotunda below me. The citizens on the first floor were going about their business, looking for the clerk's office for a marriage license or a birth certificate, walking to a courtroom to plead guilty to underage drinking, or just stopping in to use the courthouse restrooms.

There were about thirty of us standing in the foyer killing time. Half the people I recognized as police or members of the press, but I did not know the others. Were they here to testify, too? The one person I expected to see, Patti Davis, was not there.

Since Patti had begun visiting me, the police had told me nothing about the investigation. That was fine—the less I knew, the less chance there'd be that I'd slip up and tell Patti something worthwhile.

After an hour or so, John Foltz came out of the hearing room and told me to go in.

"Is it going all right?" I asked as we entered the room.

"Perfect," he answered, smiling.

I walked into a hearing room that was large, gray, and dingy. The recently completed courthouse cleanup campaign had apparently run out of paint before it reached this sad old room. It looked more like a classroom than a courtroom.

I sat in one of the half dozen school desks in the front of the room and faced the jury.

There were fifteen or twenty members scattered throughout the room, sitting in no particular order or formation. Most of them looked old, and all of them looked sick and angry. This had probably been one of the most disturbing mornings of their lives.

The attorney asked me vague, general questions—questions that called for long, rambling, anecdotal answers. Smrekar was not there, and if his court-appointed attorney was present, he did not speak. The floor was mine, and so I told my story once again, much as I had told it to the students during the prayer meeting.

The good citizens of Lincoln who were on the jury listened attentively to everything I said. I was surprised when one of the jurors asked me a question—I didn't know jurors could do that. As I talked to them, it finally dawned on me why they looked so physically ill: while most Lincoln residents were enjoying a mid-morning coffee break, they had probably been studying photographs of the bodies of Jay and Robin Fry.

Sickened or not, these elderly men and women were determined to do their duty. They listened to me with their eyes narrowed and their lips pursed. They sat up straight in their chairs, just as they probably told their grandchildren to do during holiday dinners with the family.

When I had finished talking about Smrekar, I was asked about Patti Davis. I told the jury about her involvement with Smrekar and then, as Foltz broke into a smile, I recounted the story of Patti and the fishbowl.

One day during Patti's freshman year, she had one of her numerous fights with her roommate. I don't remember what the argument was about, but to get revenge on the other girl, Patti took laundry detergent and poured it in her roommate's fishbowl, killing all the fish.

The story was not rumor. The roommate had stormed into my office and told me what had happened. When I confronted Patti, she admitted it and flashed that grin of hers at me for the first time.

Now the jury members were *mad*. One elderly woman, whose eyes had widened considerably during my testimony and who probably had bird feeders in her back yard, asked me a question. I don't remember what she asked, only that her voice quivered in anger.

As I left the hearing room, I saw Patti waiting in the foyer. She glared at me, but I smiled and waved at her. The story of Patti and the fishbowl would not, of course, be allowed in the trial itself, but the stage had been set for Patti's testimony.

That night we started to receive phone calls at home unlike any I'd ever heard. No words or voices, just strange, very ominous electronic noises. Creepy.

It dawned on me that I bet one of those animal-loving jury members asked Patti, "So what's this I hear about you and a fishbowl?"

• • •

The grand jury indicted Smrekar on nine counts of murder. I was so relieved that I never thought to ask the police how he could be charged nine times for the deaths of two people and an unborn child.

When the indictment was announced, friends called and congratulated me, as if I were a new parent or the winner of the lottery. I felt like giving everyone a cigar, or a hug, or something. I was so relieved I didn't stop to consider how strange those phone calls were.

As it happened so often in the past, my relief did not last. The grand jury's indictment did no more to finish the tension of Smrekar and my involvement with him than aspirin cures a man with a brain tumor.

The killer was in jail, not charged with all he deserved, but in jail nonetheless. The trial was set for February, and the odds for a conviction were good. Soon after the indictment, however, I began receiving death threats, and the knot in my stomach quickly reappeared.

Chapter XVII

Patti returned to my office the following Wednesday.

"I saw you at the grand jury hearing last week. You waved at me."

"Yeah." (Hey, she's not smiling.)

"What do you know about anything? What did you testify about?" She sneered. "As if I didn't know." (She was really angry this time.)

"Patti, I had to answer the questions they asked."

"I figured you'd say that."

"I don't want to be thrown into jail like Russ."

"And I bet you wouldn't wanna be thrown in jail *with* Russ either."

Silence. (We can't keep staring at each other like this.)

"You still going to keep visiting him?"

"You bet I am." She glared at me again for what seemed like a very long time, then said: "I'm going to do everything I can to get him off."

"What does that mean?"

"You'll see."

Silence.

"Still say he's innocent?"

"Course I do," she said, smiling for the first time.

"What will you do if he's found guilty?"

"He won't be."

"But if he is?"

"I just told you, Hartnett, he won't be."

Her smile gone, Patti got up and left the office.

I looked at my watch and realized we had talked for only five minutes. I had the impression she somehow knew I had told the goldfish story to the grand jury. This time Patti's anger seemed more personal, as if I had done something directly to her, which I had.

I called Tom and told him about the conversation. "So she's going to get him off, huh? She'll have a helluva time doing that."

"Was there anything in her testimony to help him?"

"Nope. She's not giving Russ an alibi like we thought. Last week one of the college girls told her advisor she knew where Patti was the night of the murders; if necessary, she said she'd testify that Russ wasn't with her.

"I think when Patti realized that—plus your goldfish story didn't make her too popular with the grand jury anyway—she chickened out and didn't give him an alibi. For all her talk about taking care of him, I think our little lady is going to let Smrekar swing in the breeze all by his lonesome."

After Tom hung up, I reconsidered Patti Davis. Up to now, I had simply dismissed her as a spoiled, homely, stupid little jerk who just made life more difficult for everyone except a cold-blooded killer. Hearing she had not helped Smrekar after all made me realize my judgment was probably simplistic.

Perhaps she was only angry with herself for failing Smrekar when he needed her, and now she was focusing her anger on me. But I didn't think so. There had been times during her freshman year when she hadn't felt threatened by authority or students more beautiful and intelligent than her, and she had been able to talk to me like the real person I hoped she was. I had forgotten all that once the murders began, but surely that person was still there.

Spoiled and stupid, yes, but more than that.

Her sneering bravado may very well have covered a frightened little girl who had traveled down a one-way street with the first man attracted to her, if he was, and now she didn't know how to come home.

• • •

A half hour later, Sarah burst into my office gasping for breath. Sarah was a vivacious, hell-raising sophomore who always burst into a room with a warm smile and happy greeting for everyone. But there was no smile this time.

"Mike," she gasped. "I just talked to Patti, and she says she's gonna kill you!"

"What?"

"Yeah, or have you killed, or something. She's really mad. I ain't never seen her like this."

"When did this happen?"

"Just now. I was sitting in my room waiting for my next class when she came in. I'm one of the few girls left on campus who talks to her, and we started talking about Russ, and she told me you were the reason why he was in all this trouble."

"Damn." (So what does that do to my theory about Patti?)

"What are you gonna do?"

"I'm not sure, Sarah. I'll have to think about it. In the meantime, though, don't tell anyone about this. I think Patti is just trying to act tough and unafraid, but I just don't know."

"You'd better be careful, Mike. She sure sounded serious to me."

Sarah, who always thought the best of everyone, was unsettled by Patti's visit. Her open, friendly, unassuming ways helped people feel and act better, and she liked them for it.

Her advisor once told me of the time she had walked into his office in the college museum one Monday morning. He was talking to the museum secretary, a kindly but strictly conservative elderly wife of a local minister. When her advisor asked the yawning Sarah how her weekend was, she brightened and said, "It was great! I ended up in Indianapolis getting laid."

I guess the secretary almost had a heart attack.

But people couldn't stay mad or shocked at Sarah for long, and soon she won over the old woman. ("I certainly can't condone many of her actions, Mr. Hartnett," she told me a few weeks later, "but she is a very nice young lady. I pray for her every night.")

They became friends, just as Sarah and Patti were friends.

But now Patti's anger had shown Sarah that some people were not as nice to others as they were to her. The look on Sarah's face was more than shocked and told me that she learned something that day.

This case was teaching all of us things we didn't want to know.

• • •

I spent the next week remembering every conversation I had had with Patti, trying to decide which Patti was real—the defensive, bratty teenager or the equal partner of a killer.

I decided I wouldn't tell anyone about her threat until I had a chance to talk to her again. That came the following Wednesday.

She walked slowly into my office looking tired and pale and sat down as if she needed the rest.

"How are you doing?"

"Okay, I guess."

"You look tired."

"Yeah, a little."

"You've sure been faithful to Russ, driving down here every week like this."

"Well, I love him, so I have to do it."

"*Have* to do it, Patti? Hell, I can remember you in this office last year complaining about dorm rules and saying you didn't *have* to do anything."

"This is different."

Silence.

"I bet Russ must be happy to see you when you drive down. Good to see a friendly face."

"Oh, Russ says he's got lots of friends in jail. They even had him sharing a cell with Michael Drabing, the guy who killed that family last summer? Russ says he and Drabing get along real good."

"I'd be scared to death to be in a cell with a killer like Drabing. How can Russ be friends with him?"

"Russ says he's real nice, and besides, Russ says it doesn't make much difference because he's getting out soon. That would just break your heart, wouldn't it?"

That was it. Hearing how wonderful Michael Drabing was and then her starting her wise-cracking again was too much. I gave myself a few seconds to compose myself by lighting a cigarette and thought, "Here goes nothing."

Quietly and deliberately I said, "Patti, I'll tell you what breaks my heart. The Frys break my heart. A couple not much older than you gets their guts splattered all over their little house. Some bastard looked 'em in the eye and butchered them. It's not fair, Patti, and it isn't a damn game.

"We're not talking about some little dorm rule like no drinking and a dopey Judicial Board asking dorm directors if they really saw some kid with a bottle in his hand. These people are dead, Patti, probably four of them, and it's not the movies where the big bad police pick on some innocent kid while his girlfriend valiantly sticks by him.

"Russ is telling you he's innocent, and you're believing him. Maybe he is, but either way, Patti, you're ruining your life for someone who, at best, robbed your girlfriends in the dorms and shoplifted meat and god knows what else.

"Everybody falls for a schmuck sometime in their lives. When I was in eighth grade, I was crazy about a girl who had an IQ of about twelve. It's no crime to fall for a dope. You try to learn from it and get on with your life. What *will* break my heart is if the killer, whoever the hell he is, isn't punished, and you throw away your life in the process."

Patti looked at me without smiling and stared down at her hands and finally said, "Maybe you're right."

She got up and walked slowly to the door. Then she turned towards me, and I saw the same old smile again. "But I don't think so." And she walked out.

● ● ●

So what the hell did that mean? I thought I was getting through to her until her dramatic exit, but I guess it was too much to ask that she admit it.

If I did just penetrate Patti's defenses, she was doing a good job of hiding it, for within an hour another acquaintance of hers came in my office reporting another death threat.

This time the student was Laura Cook, a bright, lovely, conscientious sophomore who had been Patti's resident assistant in the dorm before Patti had chosen love over education.

The story she told was almost identical to Sarah's. Patti had gone to Laura's room and told her that I was the cause of Smrekar's problems, and she would see to it that I paid for it.

So Patti's outburst the previous week to Sarah wasn't a one-time thing. She was still playing the tough guy to the people who knew her. I didn't know if she was only playing a role or if she was serious.

Despite the threats, I still couldn't believe she would carry them out. Maybe it was just a form of suicidal egotism ("No one would really want to kill *me*"), but I just didn't believe she had the same, cold-blooded nature that her boyfriend had. Despite her words, her eyes never gave me the same message that Smrekar's did.

Counselors are trained to separate their prejudices and egos from their work, but it was hard to tell if my denying her threats was my ego or if I had guessed her motives correctly. I thought I had seen a frightened little girl when I looked in her eyes, but if I was wrong, the price would be a helluva lot higher than a poor grade on a psychology exam.

I told the police about the threats, and they wanted me to press charges against her. I'm not sure why I didn't play it safe and have her arrested, but I couldn't do that, and the reasons were as complex and muddled as everything else in this case: I didn't want Sarah and Laura dragged into a case that had already proved deadly for four witnesses. I had enough on my conscience without them.

Somehow I knew if the police arrested and charged Patti, she would never have a chance to change. It would push her too far—so far that she'd never admit to herself or anyone else that she'd gone the wrong way.

Those were the least of my reasons. I knew I wasn't some naïve jerk or pious saint. I was tired of being afraid and feeling guilty about deaths unseen and threats unheard. I was sick of calling the police.

I decided to hell with it. I was sick and tired of hearing about this evil, whatever it was—this crap—but only facing it second hand.

If someone wanted to kill me, let the bastard come.

Chapter XVIII

No one came, and the threats faded away like yesterday's nightmares. Soon the murder trial preoccupied the farmers and factory workers and college students of the little town we no longer considered peaceful.

Logan County Circuit Court Judge John T. McCullough quickly ruled that Russell Albin Smrekar could not receive a fair trial in Logan County, and he was right. The town echoed with frustration and hatred for Smrekar. The same conversations were taking place in the bars and the churches and the feed stores:

"Did Smrekar really kill those Fry kids over a piece of meat?"

"What about Ruth Martin? How come the cops ain't charged him with her murder?"

"Is the son of a bitch gonna get off with his life like Drabing did?" (He would, of course, because the state of Illinois had no death penalty at the time.)

The trial was moved to Sullivan, a small farming community fifty miles southeast of Lincoln and the seat of Moultrie County. That pleased Smrekar's counsel, a middle-aged lawyer in a wheelchair who had inherited the case when the usual court-appointed defense attorney declined it. That attorney had already defended Smrekar on the shoplifting charge, which had never been resolved because the witnesses kept disappearing and dying.

The lawyers selected a jury on Tuesday in less than six hours—farmers, a truck driver, factory workers, the owner of a supply company, a housewife, and a county employee. The prosecuting attorney warned them they would have to view "horrible and nauseating" color photographs, and the defense attorney, according to one report, made certain that no pregnant women were seated.

I had seen the courthouse before while driving through town to a basketball game. It looked like Lincoln's big, old, courthouse sitting peacefully in a tranquil town square. It was Sullivan's first murder trial in thirty years, and the Logan County Sheriff's deputies, who were still in charge of the trial even though it had been moved, frisked everyone before allowing them to enter the courtroom—just as the big city police did and the textbooks told them to.

The weather was hot for late February on the windswept Illinois prairie. The *Lincoln Courier* reporter described the scene as if he were covering the Scopes trial fifty years and 500 miles ago: "As temperatures soared to the high fifties outside, ladies fanned themselves, and men shifted uncomfortably, perspiring both from anticipation and the weather."

The stage was set, but I was not there to watch it. I was told to be prepared to testify on twenty-four hours' notice, and President Stoltz would have allowed me to attend the trial every day if I'd asked him. But a kind of lethargy set in, something I can't explain even years later.

I guess I was tired. There had been so many times when my efforts seemed to result in more fear, more death, and no end to it all. The case appeared to be coming to an end, but in a way I was too sick to watch it. I didn't want to see the "horrible and nauseating" slides because I had seen them in my own mind too often.

I didn't want to hear the prosecutor make innuendoes about the disappearances of Mike Mansfield and Ruth Martin; I had made enough of them myself. I heard that Smrekar was going to testify in his own behalf, but I had already heard his lies to the Judicial Board what seemed like a decade earlier.

There were reasons to attend, I guess. I could have finally learned what kind of case the police actually had against the former Lincoln College student, which the papers kept calling him, as if we'd given birth to him with a bloody shotgun clutched in his hands.

I could see what he looked like with his hair neatly trimmed. I could see the Fry relatives and Ruth Martin's husband. I could see how Smrekar's lawyer cross-examined the state's witnesses, so I could be better prepared when my turn came. I could see how valiantly Patti defended her lover. I could see and hear and feel it all first-hand. I could go to the trial and learn, but I already knew too much.

Instead I sat in my office and learned about the trial through the media, just like the other townsfolk. I sat in my office and tried to counsel troubled students, hushing them whenever the local news came over the radio.

● ● ●

The prosecution began its case with the star witness, Jay Fry's sister and next-door neighbor, Ann. She told the court she was watching television late that night when she heard Jay and Robin pull up in their truck about 1:15 AM. She looked out her window and saw them walking to the front door. She noticed that they had left the dome light on in their truck, so she opened the window and told them. Then she turned back to her television.

Soon she heard a loud roar. Thinking it was an auto accident, she looked out her window once again. All was quiet except for the barking of their German Shepherds.

As she was turning back to her television, she saw a man wearing jeans and a dark stocking cap that covered most of his shoulder-length hair standing in the Fry's front yard As she watched, he suddenly stopped and acted as if he had forgotten something. He turned, walked into the Fry home, and turned on the dining room light. Why? We don't know for certain.

Ann ran to the phone and called her brother. No answer. She looked out the window and saw the Fry home was dark once again. Again she called.

No answer. She quickly woke her husband, Clarence, and they ran next door. As she opened the front door, a box of shotgun shells was lying on the floor. Then she saw Robin sprawled on the living room floor in a pool of blood. Jay was lying next to her. "His head was split down the middle," she said.

Ann ran home and called the police. When they arrived, they found her in the yard between the two homes, crying. "I saw who did it," she sobbed. "I saw who killed them."

She could not identify the killer, though, until she had sessions with a hypnotist. Ann had been hypnotized three times in an effort to help her remember the face of the killer. Her last visit to the physician was October 17, the day before she identified Smrekar.

She testified that it was Russell Albin Smrekar who had gunned down her brother and his wife. "I would stake my life on it."

Smrekar's attorney questioned Ann about the lighting conditions that night, suggesting that she could not have seen anyone well enough to identify him days later. The prosecution countered with testimony by one of the detectives, who talked about the streetlight, the short distance between the two homes, and concluded that it was bright enough "to read a book by."

My affable detective friend also presented his slide show of Jay's and Robin's bodies. I'm glad I wasn't there to see them. The *Lincoln Courier* reporter called the slides "graphic," but he did not say if they made the jury members as angry and tight-lipped and ashen as the grand jury had been. Perhaps the reporter too was fighting the growing nausea in his stomach and didn't notice the jury's reaction.

When I read that in the paper, I immediately began thinking the case might be thrown out since there was no defense attorney present when Ann was hypnotized. It seemed like judges, with far weaker grounds than this, were overturning convictions and letting killers go free.

Later I thought, why would a defense attorney be present? No one had been charged, so who would need a defense attorney?

• • •

So Ann had been hypnotized, and no one knew if her testimony would help send Smrekar to prison or get him off. We all hoped the trial would answer questions and let us get on with our lives. It was quickly apparent, however, that Smrekar's lawyer would use the hypnosis issue as a major ground for appeal. Whatever else happened in the trial, and no matter how conclusive it would be, the case would not end here.

The prosecution had more to offer than a hypnotized witness. There were other witnesses, all thoughtfully provided by Smrekar himself.

The first was a Jimmy Cooper, Jr., who was serving a two to ten year sentence for aggravated battery. He had been awaiting trial in the Macon County jail and testified that he would sit in his cell and listen to Drabing and Smrekar brag to each other about their murders.

Cooper told the court that Smrekar laughed about killing Jay Fry over a piece of meat. He wasn't going to let Fry's testimony send him to jail, so he killed him—and he killed Robin because she just happened to be there. He told Cooper that he had entered the house through the back door with a 12-gauge pump-action shotgun. And waited. When the Frys returned home, Smrekar bragged to Cooper, Jay had lunged for his collection of rifles, but Smrekar shot him. Cooper quoted Smrekar as saying, "I blew his head off."

Then Cooper said Smrekar turned to Robin, much as I had imagined, and shot her, too.

Cooper also claimed Smrekar bragged that he killed Ruth Martin and someone else whom Smrekar didn't name. On another question, Cooper said that Smrekar bragged about having had Mike Mansfield killed.

Cellmates weren't the only people who overheard Smrekar bragging. A Macon County deputy sheriff testified that when he was booking Smrekar on October 19, he commented about the seriousness of the charges. Smrekar agreed, then started to laugh. "They'll have to prove it," Smrekar told him.

The officer said he told Smrekar it wasn't funny, but Smrekar turned away and in a low voice said, "I did it, but they'll have to prove it."

When I read the paper that evening, I was very thankful that Smrekar had remained such a braggart.

Cooper was eventually moved and replaced in the cell by a James Kennedy, an accused rapist. But Smrekar kept on bragging. Kennedy said Smrekar was excited by all the publicity generated by the murders and avidly read every account he could. Patti would send him clippings about the case, and sometimes she would copy news stories verbatim in her letters. Once he told Kennedy, "I did it all, but they'll never prove it."

Apparently Smrekar did more than just kill four people, shoplift meat, burglarize dorm rooms, and rob police stations. Kennedy added, "He discussed cases with me that aren't even before this court."

When I read all this in the paper, I should have been pleased. The state was proving the case, and as the prosecution's case was coming to an end, it looked like I wouldn't have to testify after all.

Kennedy had more to say: he told the small-town courtroom that he thought he was going to beat the rape charge and be set free. He said Smrekar made him an offer if he was, in fact, let out of jail soon. Smrekar had more than $6,000 saved from various unmentioned jobs. Good ole, faithful Patti was holding the money for him. He told Kennedy that if he would kill Ann, Jay Fry's sister, Smrekar would tell Patti to give him $3,000. Kill the eyewitness, and once Smrekar read about the murder in the newspaper, the money was his.

Kennedy's testimony was damaging to Smrekar, but not encouraging to me. All I could think was, "Who does Kennedy have to kill to get the rest of the money?"

• • •

There were other witnesses, but none as damaging to Smrekar as Ann and the convicts. Each served to slam the prison door a little tighter.

A state trooper testified that he gave Smrekar a speeding ticket at 3:00 AM, the morning after the murders. He said he clocked Smrekar driving ninety-five miles an hour on Interstate 55. Smrekar was driving north near Odell, a small town far south of his home in Joliet. This didn't prove he committed the murders, but it did prove that he could have been in Lincoln when Jay and Robin died.

Paul Martin, Ruth's husband, testified, but it didn't have much bearing on whether Smrekar pulled the trigger against Jay and Robin. Later, when a pathologist testified that Jay had died when his brain was "totally evacuated from his head," I wondered about Paul Martin, sitting in court listening to a scientist speak rationally and calmly about someone's brains splattered about a living room. How had Paul Martin, once a suspect in his wife's disappearance, watched as Smrekar listened impassively to the pathologist? Had it prompted him to wonder about the fate of his wife?

Patti testified.

She said she did not know where Smrekar was that night. Yes, she had copied news stories about the murders and sent them to him, her true love. Yes, the scrap of paper Smrekar had given James Kennedy when he proposed murder for hire had her phone number on it. But no, she did not know where Smrekar was the night of the murders.

All the brave talk about doing whatever was necessary to save her lover meant nothing. Patti had looked the judicial system in the eye and blinked.

• • •

Finally, the prosecution called the hypnotist, Dr. Dean Hauter, who had practiced medicine in San Jose (pronounced "San Joe's" in this part of the world), yet another small town near Lincoln, for thirty years. He was accredited by the American Medical Association and the American Society of Clinical Hypnosis.

He said he had three sessions with Ann Mardis and that he had not used any post-hypnotic suggestions with her. The final session was held the day before Ann identified Smrekar. There was no defense attorney present during the sessions. Why would there be if no one had been charged?

Chapter XIX

The clear, strong case against Smrekar might have fallen apart if Ann's testimony was thrown out on appeal. Without her brave, sad story, all the state had proven was Smrekar bragged to friends and drove his car too fast—not exactly capital offenses.

As I thought back on those first dorm burglaries years ago, I couldn't stop remembering Smrekar's response to being accused. He had continued to burglarize dorm rooms long after he knew he was a suspect. He believed his claim of innocence was enough that I'd let him stay in school and the police would go away. He agreed to take a lie detector test. He robbed the police station. He bragged to cellmates about Jay Fry's trophies even though that information had never been released. He told Patti he would be a free man and get his money back from Lincoln College.

He kept digging himself a deeper hole, and he continued to think he was immune. As word came that the defense was beginning its case, I hoped Smrekar would keep thinking the same way.

Smrekar's cousin, Cheryl Pasdirtz from Joliet, took the stand and testified that she had watched television with Smrekar the evening before the early-morning murders. She said that, while her husband slept, she and Russ watched *Bonnie and Clyde* until after midnight. He left her home about 12:45 AM. She did not hear from him until he called her the next day to tell her about the speeding ticket. If what she said was true, Smrekar could not have driven to Lincoln, even at ninety-five miles an hour, and killed the Frys by 1:15.

The testimony would have been effective if it wasn't so different from the story she first told the police.

During his cross examination, the prosecutor forced Pasdirtz to admit that she originally told the police her husband watched the film with them, and he and Smrekar had talked to each other throughout the evening. Pasdirtz also admitted telling police that her aunt had told her about Smrekar's speeding ticket.

Cheryl Pasdirtz cried when confronted with these conflicting stories. She said she had lied to the police then but "was telling the truth now."

"I was told on repeated occasions that if Russ was convicted, I'd be in trouble, too." She said she wouldn't lie under oath because "I have a husband and four children at home." But her credibility was gone.

So another of Smrekar's friends had failed him. Mike Mansfield, who had faithfully hidden the records from the robbery, had eventually tried to turn state's evidence. Patti visited Russ faithfully and sent him newspaper articles, but she was no help on the witness stand. His friends in jail, with the exception of Michael Drabing, told the world about his claims of easy murders. Now his cousin, who probably agreed to help him, little knowing what the true case was, was hedging her bets.

• • •

I was sitting in my office talking to a freshman on the morning that a faculty member stuck his head in the doorway and told me Smrekar would be testifying that afternoon. The freshman, a pretty young woman from Chicago, and I resumed our conversation, but apparently I wasn't paying much attention.

After trying to talk to me for a few more minutes, she finally stopped and said, "Mr. Hartnett, you ain't listening."

"I'm sorry Delitha. I'm thinking about a murder trial that's going on now. It doesn't have anything to do with school—not anymore, at least—but I'm a little worried about it."

"Shoot," she scoffed. "Don't you be worrying about one little murder trial." She shook her head and with a wry smile added, "In my neighborhood back home, you'd be worried all the time."

• • •

Since there was no one else to help him, Smrekar took the stand in front of a quiet, crowded courtroom. His story was the same as his cousin's latest version. After watching *Bonnie and Clyde*, Smrekar left Cheryl's home around 12:30 and decided to drive towards Kankakee. He said he missed all three Kankakee exits on the interstate, and that's why he ended up speeding near Odell.

After receiving the speeding ticket, he drove to a park in Kankakee, checked out camping sights, then drove home. "It was typical for me to take my car out on weekends and do that."

He denied bragging to his cellmates about the murders. He claimed they read the details in the newspapers and in Patti's letters and lied about hearing them from him.

He denied bragging about the murders to the sheriff's deputy. He didn't kill Jay and Robin Fry. He didn't kill

Ruth Martin. He didn't offer money to kill Ann Mardis. He didn't do anything, except speed.

Smrekar remained calm and rather pleasant, if distant, and seemed unaware of what his testimony was doing to him. He still thought his word was enough to make the court forget.

He didn't seem to realize that his story raised more questions than it answered. Why, after a leisurely night of television, did he have a sudden urge to drive like hell down the interstate? How could he miss three highway exits so close to home? Why check camping sites in the dark? How could his cellmates know details about Jay Fry's trophies, if not from him? Why had he and his cousin originally claimed they had watched TV with her husband?

One of his answers was typical of the case and of him: when asked if it was unusual for him to drive so far and so fast from home, Smrekar looked at the jury and said, "To be caught, yes." And he smiled.

• • •

The prosecution's closing argument was perfunctory; it did not need to be any other way. The defense summary was desperate, based on questions rather than facts. Could Ann Mardis really have seen Smrekar's face? Would Cheryl Pasdirtz really lie? There's nothing felonious about speeding on the interstate, is there? Can the jury really trust the testimony of two convicted felons? The defense never attempted to explain how Kennedy could have known about Smrekar's exploits.

Both lawyers talked of the motive in their final efforts to sway the jury. The prosecutor said, "These murders were the most frightening, brutal acts of crime committed in this part of Illinois in a long time. They were planned executions. Smrekar was in the process of eliminating witnesses."

The defense tried to refute that claim with a question: "Why would a man charged with petty theft risk a murder conviction? Use your life's experiences. He's no fool."

The jury began deliberating at 5:15 that afternoon, and before the lawyers could finish their sandwiches, the verdict was announced: Guilty on all counts. Ann Mardis and her mother and Patti Davis and Cheryl Pasdirtz wept.

Judge McCullough quieted the courtroom and asked each member of the jury if that was his or her verdict. "Yes," answered the housewife, the truck driver, and the others.

After setting April 1 as the date for sentencing, McCullough insisted Smrekar be led away before allowing anyone else to leave. The four women continued to cry.

As Smrekar was being escorted away in handcuffs, Patti cried out, "I love you, Russ!"

Smrekar stopped, turned towards her, and smiled. "I'll be back," he said. "Don't worry about it."

• • •

The phone rang all night long. People called to congratulate Barb and me as if we'd just won an election, broken an athletic record, or had a baby. These friends knew Barbara and I would be relieved, and they wanted to share it with us. Even Delitha called: "Didn't I tell you not to worry? You listen to me more often, Mr. Hartnett, you'd be in better shape. Now don't you be worrying no more, you understand?"

As I walked Sam down the dark streets that night, however, the fear was still there. I thought if there was any truth to Patti's threats, the verdict might make her angry enough to . . . Would this feeling ever go away? Sam and I snuck from tree to tree and finally ran home.

• • •

Everyone was back in court on April Fool's Day to hear the sentence. I was tempted to drive to the courtroom to gloat and listen to Patti cry and see Smrekar in handcuffs. I thought that if I heard the sentence and saw him lose his freedom, it might end it for me.

The same lethargy that paralyzed me during the trial took hold again, however, and I said, "To hell with it." Besides, being there probably wouldn't have made any difference.

Before the sentencing, the defense submitted motions for a new trial. All denied. One of them dealt with the short time the jury took to reach a verdict. "Hardly time for more than three ballots," the defense complained. A jury's speed is not a problem when the evidence is clear, Judge McCullough claimed. "As a member of that jury, I would not have taken any longer to return a verdict."

The prosecution asked for a sentence tough enough to be a "flag" to future parole boards, so Smrekar "should never be let back into society to commit this kind of crime again."

Judge McCullough listened to the lawyers and sentenced Smrekar to one hundred to three hundred years in prison for each murder, to be served consecutively.

He said, "Society really doesn't have a place for a Russell Smrekar. You have attempted to conduct a one-man war against this system, and you made a pretty good effort, but not good enough. There's no doubt in the court's mind that these crimes were premeditated and well thought out. Hopefully, future parole boards and law enforcement agencies will remember this crime and the trauma it caused, not only to the families, but to the entire community of Logan County, so that this man will never be released in society again."

Smrekar was led away to begin serving his sentence. He would be eligible for parole in nine years.

Chapter XX

Finally, finally, it was over! I was so relieved the next morning—until the phone rang. It was the police asking me to arrange a meeting of all the "townie" female students. That afternoon, about thirty young women crowded into my office so Bill and Tom could talk to them. Here's why:

They had received a phone call from a woman who refused to give her name. She said her daughter had been parked with her boyfriend near the construction site for the interstate highway, and they may have seen someone bury something. The daughter wasn't supposed to be parked with her boyfriend, so she hadn't told her mother until she read about the Smrekar trial in the newspaper and realized she may have seen Smrekar bury Ruth Martin's body.

"Look," the detectives told the young women in my office, "you're not going to be a witness; all we want is another phone call giving more specific directions so we know where to dig."

The young women had blank stares on their faces, and no one said a word.

When the detectives left they said they were going over to Lincoln Christian College with the same message to those students.

No one ever called the police.

• • •

A yawning Len Branson shuffled into my office one morning soon after the trial. Long before he became Smrekar's dorm director, Len stopped going to bed at night. He resisted that idea during his first year in the dorm, but finally decided it was easier to stay up all night prepared to talk or confiscate beer or quiet arguments than it was to lie in bed wondering what the kids were up to. So Len had become a night owl, like many of the students and a few of the night-shift police who would often drop in for coffee and conversation.

"I heard something from the boys in blue a while back I didn't want to tell you about before," Len said with a tired grin. "You wanna hear it now?"

"Lemme guess: one of your guys got the mayor's daughter pregnant?"

"Hell, I would have told you that right away."

"Your third floor's started a devil worship cult?"

"Nope."

"Everybody in the dorm's having a sex change operation, and it'll be a women's dorm next year?"

Len shook his head.

"Okay, so tell me."

"Remember the money Smrekar offered that guy Kennedy to kill Jay Fry's sister, money Patti was saving for him?"

"Yeah. So?"

"Yeah, well it never came out in the trial because I guess it wasn't relevant, but Kennedy told police Smrekar offered him money to kill you, too. The police thought it was bullshit and didn't want you to worry, so they didn't say anything. You were worried enough in those days."

So there it was. Smrekar hadn't forgotten about me.

"That sounds like something I had a right to know."

"Sure it is. But what the hell would you have done? You wouldn't have left town or anything. You would have stayed, kept coming to work, and worried more."

Len was right. He ambled off to bed a few minutes later, and I decided if I started thinking about what he said, I wouldn't get any work done. I forced myself to concentrate on next fall's campus movie schedule. That worked until I came to *Bonnie & Clyde* in one of the movie catalogs, and I knew I couldn't avoid it any longer. I closed the catalog, lit another cigarette, and thought about it all once again.

So why was I still alive? Because Kennedy never left jail? Was Smrekar just acting tough and didn't mean it? Because Patti wouldn't cooperate?

Like so many other questions, I had no answers. But unlike the others, I realized with some surprise that I didn't care that much anymore. The paralysis that had kept me away from the trial had sunk deeper, like a shot of Novocain. I was aware that something was working on me, maybe gnawing away at me, but I couldn't feel it.

If anyone had been watching, they would have thought I shrugged my shoulders as I turned back to the movie schedule. I told Barbara about Len's message that night. She didn't seem to feel it either, or so I thought.

A few months later, my editor at the Bloomington *Pantagraph* and his wife visited us, and he and I started toying with the idea of my going to the prison and interviewing Smrekar.

"No!" Barbara shouted. "You will NOT see him again!" Decades of marriage, I had never seen Barbara so adamant. The interview idea was quickly abandoned.

I guess the news that Smrekar may have wanted me dead affected Barbara more than I had thought.

• • •

The town quickly reverted back to normal, but under the façade of the proud-to-live-here citizens was a little less pride, a little less assurance that their town was somehow better than most. Michael Drabing and Russell Smrekar had robbed them of that, and it would take a long time, if ever, for them to regain it.

The verdict had caused celebrations and complaints. Joy that the right man had been convicted, and anger that Illinois had no death penalty to give him.

There was also frustration. As a friend said over breakfast at the Gem Lunch one Saturday morning, "Why doesn't Smrekar just tell the cops where Ruth's body is? They can't do any more to him now, and at least her family could bury her and try to get over it all."

Barbara, who had always analyzed Smrekar better than anyone, had the answer. "Because that's all Smrekar's got left. He tried to beat the system and was thrown in jail for it. How else does he avoid thinking he lost? He's got nothing else to show for his trouble, no other way to make the system suffer."

There was hope, too. No one knew much about prison, but we heard convicts thought killers of pregnant women were the second lowest form of life, only above child molesters. There was hope that the killers, rapists, and armed robbers in Illinois prisons would make Smrekar suffer in ways the state could not.

No one could dwell on Smrekar for too long except, perhaps, for the victims' relatives. There was nothing new to think, nothing more to say.

Soon the spring rains came—or didn't come, I forget which—and the farmers' complaints turned from the justice system to their drought-stricken, soaked, or unplanted crops. The townspeople were probably a little more leery than usual about those rambunctious kids over at the college, but they never complained directly to us. In fact, no one ever said it was the college's fault that three of their own had been murdered, that if Lincoln College had never accepted Smrekar, Jay and Robin and Ruth would still be alive. They must have thought it, though. I know I did.

The crime rate went back to normal, too. But the county built a fancy million-dollar jail that's much tougher to break into, just in case.

The prayer meetings continued each Friday, much happier affairs as graduation crept closer and sophomores discussed their plans for the future. As the nights wore on and the drinks took effect, at least one student would get emotional and misty-eyed and confess to us all how much his Lincoln College "family" meant to him. Then a classmate would hug him, and the topic would change, and there would be dancing and laughter and more plans and dreams until someone else would stop and say, "Goddammit, I'm sure gonna miss this" and it would start all over again.

Graduation that year was not the standard hugs and thank-yous and promises to write. A few students—those who knew the Smrekar story, those who warned me of the danger in the fall and congratulated me on the lack of it in the spring, those who listened to Patti's boasts and empty threats—were hugged a little tighter than the rest.

• • •

The following August, I took a break one afternoon during new-student orientation and went next door to the bookstore to buy a birthday card. I had just taken one out of the rack when I heard that voice again, still slow and pointed and barely holding back a sneer.

"Hello, Mr. Hartnett."

I turned around and dropped the birthday card. I earn my living talking to students, but this time I was speechless.

"Surprised to see me?" Patti asked.

I closed my mouth and nodded.

"Well don't worry; I'm not gonna stay long and spoil your pretty little school. I got a cousin who's a freshman, so I thought I'd come down and show her around."

I don't remember the rest of the conversation, just that it was superficial. As soon as Patti said, "See you around, Mike" and left the bookstore, I ran back to my office and called President Stoltz. He said he'd call the police. I said, "Fine, I don't want to go near her. You handle it," and my hand was shaking when I hung up.

Stoltz had the dean order Patti off campus, and the next day I was deluged with questions from faculty members—the only ones left on campus who remembered her:

"Did she threaten you?"

"No."

"Still see Russ?"

"I didn't ask."

"What's she doing now?"

"I don't know."

"She still fat?"

"Yeah."

I have not seen Patti since that busy afternoon in the bookstore. I'm curious about what's happened to her, and what she did with Smrekar's money, but not curious enough to do anything about it.

• • •

The search for Ruth Martin's body finally ended. There seemed to be nowhere else to look. The consensus in town was that Ruth was buried under a cornfield or beneath one of the new sections of the interstate that was replacing old Route 66. The seasons wore on, and the farmers plowed and harvested, and the final sections of the highway were completed amid the usual politicians' hoopla.

Then in February of 1978, a reporter for the NBC television station in Springfield received a letter from an inmate in one of the Illinois prisons. In it, he claimed he knew the location of Ruth's body. When questioned further, the prisoner said Michael Drabing told him he knew where Smrekar had buried the body. Drabing wouldn't tell the prisoner the exact location but gave him two clues and told it to figure it out for himself. The two clues were "McLane" and "M for Mom."

The riddle eventually led the reporter and police officials from the three counties to a prairie cemetery outside McLean, a small town between Lincoln and Bloomington, the town where Ruth's car had been found with bloodstains in the trunk.

At the cemetery, a check of the records showed that two people had been buried there in late May of 1976, just days before Ruth disappeared. The two graves were only a few plots from one another and between them was a family plot with a headstone inscribed, "McLane." To the rear of the plot was another headstone, this time with "McLane" on one side and "Mom" on the other. The long search seemed to be over.

Armed with a search warrant signed by Judge McCullough, the police erected a huge tent over the sight and brought in heaters to thaw the ground, frozen by a record-breaking winter. Finally they began digging, an inch at a time, looking for a woman whose only crime was driving into a grocery store parking lot.

They found nothing.

Paul Martin, Ruth's husband, died of cancer in May 1983. Ruth Martin was still missing.

• • •

In that same cold February in 1978, the case made the pages of *Official Detective* magazine. The February issue covered the major points of the murders, but the editors chose not to highlight the story on the cover. Instead, they chose "Incredible Blood Lust of the Washington Parolee" and "Did Conscience Make the Sex Fiend Kill Four More?" But back on page 76, between the murder of the mother of fourteen children and another murder in North Carolina, was the headline, "Dead Witnesses Tell No Tales." The story was somewhat complete and included photos of Jay and Robin—and Russell Albin Smrekar with short hair and handcuffs.

The newsstand in town sold out. I wondered at the time if Ann Mardis or Paul Martin bought copies, or even Patti Davis for that matter.

• • •

My job was easier that first year after Smrekar's conviction. There had always been an air of crisis about my duties, no time for long-range planning, just barely enough to put out brush fires. To the students, of course, everything was a crisis. Now I knew what a real crisis was, and the normal day-to-day emergencies just didn't seem as important as they had before a guitar and a few albums were stolen from a campus dorm room.

The chemistry between the students and me didn't seem quite as strong, but that was no doubt due to a change in me, not the students. During these first few months of the school year, the highs weren't as gratifying, but the lows didn't seem so bad, either.

I tried to work with the deans to give the students a little more of what they paid for, a little more of what we had promised them. Perhaps, because the chemistry wasn't as good anymore, or I was just tired, I spent less time playing the political games and more time just telling the deans they were wrong about one thing or another—or was it one thing after another?

The deans didn't seem to hear me; I guess I wasn't a team player anymore.

The antics of the administration replaced some of the emotions caused by the students; by the end of the year, the lows had returned, but the highs hadn't.

I kept busy, busy enough to keep most of the memories away, although occasionally something—a tone of voice, a glance, an image—would remind me of a piece of the puzzle or a question left unanswered. As I struggled through the year, I first began thinking maybe it was time to leave Lincoln College. But the emotional paralysis stayed, for the most part, intact, until graduation.

Chapter XXI

My relationship with the deans continued to deteriorate. By the spring of 1979, I was sending out resumes long before the deans announced yet another administrative reorganization that included only team players. I accepted the *Administrator of the Year* award from the sophomore class at their year-end banquet and looked for another job. Many of my friends left at the same time, including the dorm directors, so even if I had stayed, I would have missed part of what had been so good about the place.

The job had been wearing me down ever since the murders; the students and I still had a rapport, but it was no longer a great rapport; it wasn't what it had been. After the murders, Barbara wasn't as eager to drive a two-lane Illinois road fifty miles each way to work, especially the last two miserable winters. We determined we should move to Peoria, closer to Barbara's college, whether or not there were late-night dorm emergencies that had kept us living close to campus.

I had been writing part-time for the newspaper in Bloomington during my last year in Lincoln, and since there were no education jobs available at the time in Peoria, I sent my clips to area magazines and newspapers. A trade magazine hired me as assistant editor, and we moved to a home twenty minutes from Barbara's college.

To put it another way, we stepped off the emotional roller coaster.

Most of the others involved with Russell Smrekar are gone or changed. Detective Bill Krueger retired from the Lincoln Police Department in 1980, became chief of police in Salem, Illinois, and later retired to Florida. He wrote his own book about the case, *A Force for Evil: Assassination in a Small Town* (Authorhouse, 2003).

Somehow Coach Al Pickering, without my assistance on the scorebook, managed to win two state basketball championships and place ninth and second in national tournaments.

Bob Patterson, one of the dorm directors, went into corrections work and eventually was elected sheriff of Logan County.

While he was working on his Ph.D. in accounting, Len Branson, Smrekar's dorm director, took a job as manager of the Holiday Inn in Bloomington, where Ruth Martin's bloody car had been found. He recently retired as head of the Accounting Department at the University of Illinois, Springfield.

I was told that every year, Ann, Jay Fry's sister, wrote a letter to the *Lincoln Courier* thanking people for remembering her brother and sister-in-law. Ann died in 2012. She was sixty-five. Her obituary said donations should be made to the Special Olympics and the Multiple Sclerosis Foundation.

To the horror of all of us, Pete Andrews decided to remodel the Gem Lunch. Although the wonderful wooden booths with forty years of gum underneath the tables were replaced with plastic ones, the food and the feelings were as good as ever.

Before I left town, I convinced Pete to donate the old booths to the college student union. The maintenance staff installed the booths and when it was apparent there was one too many, I stole it.

It was in our kitchen for years. We ate in the Gem so often during our years in Lincoln that we no doubt sat at that same booth and talked about the murders over bacon and eggs. Sitting there now, remembering it all over a slow Saturday breakfast surrounded by the dark wooden booth walls, the only things missing are the friends who have gone on to other things, and that red grape Pete used to plop on the plate.

Chapter XXII

Barbara and I moved from Lincoln to Washington, Illinois, a Peoria suburb, in 1979, and I began learning my new profession. I was the assistant editor of *Profitable Craft Merchandising*, a trade (business) magazine for the arts-and-crafts industry. I didn't know what an assistant editor did, what a trade magazine was, or anything about arts and crafts.

Obviously, I had a lot to learn.

My head and my heart, though, were filled with memories of the murders and guilt. I knew many elements that were never made public, and I wanted to write about them. I didn't, because I didn't know how to start. Was this a first-person story—a memoir—or was it a third-person, true-crime piece?

Shortly after we moved, a friend gave me a book, saying, "This is a great piece of writing, and it is set in Lincoln." I read the book, *So Long, See You Tomorrow*, by William Maxwell. It's written in memoir style, and the main character is on the periphery of a murder in Lincoln who comes away feeling guilty.

That's me!

In addition to being an award-winning novelist, Mr. Maxwell was also the fiction editor of *The New Yorker*, so I wrote my one-and-only fan letter, telling him how much I enjoyed his book and gave him a short synopsis of my story.

A few days later I received a letter from him:

Dear Mr. Hartnett,

What a horrifying story! I see no reason why you shouldn't write it, if and when you feel inclined to. In any case, it will take you into a confrontation with the nature of evil, about which next to nothing is known, really.

I'm glad you liked my book. I'm not much for lunching and dining because they both interfere with my duties to my typewriter, but it would be nice to meet you over a cup of coffee or whatever. So do call me when you are in New York.

> Yours sincerely,
> William Maxwell

A few months later I was in New York covering an industry event, and Mr. Maxwell insisted I visit him at his apartment on the Upper East Side. He greeted me at the door in his pajamas and bathrobe and said he wasn't feeling well, so could we talk in the bedroom so he could lay down?

I offered to return another time when he felt better, but he insisted, so I followed him to the bedroom. He lay down, I pulled up a chair, and we talked for about three hours.

He was adamant that I write a memoir and not a third-person piece. "Anyone," he said, "with the time and the money could go to Lincoln, interview everyone, and write, in effect, a report. No one could write your story but you."

That conversation was truly one of the highlights of my life. Here was a great writer who had worked with the top writers of the last half of the twentieth century, sick in bed, and he spent three hours talking to the assistant editor of a trade magazine from Peoria!

When I returned home, I woke up early every weekday morning for about a year and wrote a rough draft of what you've read thus far. Then three things happened: I was promoted to editor, which meant a lot more work and travel—and I was still learning this new profession. About the same time, the office hours changed; instead of working 9:00 to 5:00, it meant 8:00 to 4:00. So, to keep writing, instead of waking up at 5:00 each weekday morning to write, I'd have to get up at 4:00.

I also realized that my burning desire to get the story, my story, down on paper had waned a bit. Writing the story had exorcised some of my guilt. Just some.

So I put the manuscript away—for about thirty-five years.

• • •

What you've just read in the first twenty-one chapters was written in the early 1980s. What's happened since?

A few years into the 1980s, Ruth Martin's daughter, Ann Hancock, called me. She had heard from a mutual friend that I was working on a book about the murders. It was a long, sad conversation. She was very bitter about the police. She believed that the pressure they put on her father hastened his eventual illness and death.

I understood her anger, but I understood the police, too. The majority of married murder victims were killed by their spouses, so of course her dad would be the first person they suspected.

Ann wrote to me in 1984, wondering if I had finished the book. She wrote it from where she worked, Emmet Field School in Love, Kentucky. Years later, as I was closing in on the finish, I went online to the school's website to see if she was still employed there. No sign of her, so I contacted the principal to see if she had Ann's contact information. She did not. Apparently, Ann had left the school before the principal arrived.

So she's out there, somewhere.

• • •

In the spring of 2010, Barbara and I were having dinner in Lincoln with Paul and Sue Beaver. Paul was a retired history professor at Lincoln College. With them was a friend who hadn't been in Lincoln in forty years or so and knew nothing about the murders.

We were eating at Guzzardo's Italian Villa, a popular, crowded restaurant on the town square. I was about half-way through telling Paul's friend about the murders when someone tapped me on the shoulder.

A young man was standing there. What happened next happened so quickly; I'm just guessing about his age: Thirty? Thirty-five? His voice was shaking: "PLEASE DON'T TALK ABOUT THIS, PLEASE! IT'S STILL TOO PAINFUL!"

Then he turned and walked away. He had to have been a very young boy, if he was alive at all, when the murders happened.

• • •

In 2011 Smrekar was suffering from a terminal illness and admitted to killing Ruth Martin and Mike Mansfield. The police brought him back to Lincoln, and he tried to remember where he'd buried Ruth's body. Yes, he had buried her at the interstate construction site decades ago. He couldn't pinpoint the location; it was dark when he buried her, and the entire area had been completely developed decades ago.

He never said anything about the location of Mike Mansfield's remains.

When asked why he hadn't confessed earlier, he said he thought he would get a pardon for his murder convictions. He was fifty-six when he died.

A few days after his death I received a phone call from Phil Barrile, a detective for the Rolling Meadows Police Department. All these years later, he was still looking at the case, still in touch with Mike Mansfield's family.

Like the conversation with Ruth Martin's daughter, it was long and sad. It could have been taken out of the old *Cold Case* television series.

• • •

As for Lincoln College itself, it went through some very hard times until Dr. Jack Nutt became president. Our friends in Lincoln tell us Jack may very well have saved the college from going under. He finally retired and passed away.

Two others were president, and today Dr. David Gerlach is president, and he is leading Lincoln College back to its roots, redeveloping a four-year college structure.

Now Lincoln College offers a number of four-year programs culminating in bachelor degrees. (The vast majority of the students I knew in the 1970s would have loved to have stayed another two years.)

And the campus looks wonderful. It always did, but now there's a new gymnasium, dormitory, and student union.

• • •

In 2013 we retired and moved to Lawrence, Kansas, to be closer to relatives. Now, at last, I have time to finish my book.

It wasn't so easy, however, to immerse myself back into that depressing, scary time. Plus, there was the drudgery of typing one-hundred, plus, pages into the computer. That problem was solved, however, by hiring a college student to type it for me.

Now I'm close to finishing the manuscript! Well, no. In 2016 I received another call from detective Barrile. He tracked me down in Kansas to tell me there had been a new development in the case. He couldn't tell me what it was, but did I remember a particular student? I recognized the name but didn't remember anything about the student.

A few days later I read media reports that police, some in hazmat suits, descended on a house that, decades ago, was owned by Smrekar's mother's sister. They found nothing, but said they were still working on new leads.

So I put the manuscript aside *again*. Maybe there would be another chapter to write.

Months passed, and no word from detective Barrile. I emailed him, and he said yes, he was still working on the case.

I have to finish this, however. I'm getting old, and this has been hanging over my head for more than forty years. Time for me to stop, even if there will be another chapter.

For years, the Russell Smrekar drama made me an interesting guest at cocktail parties—at least for a few minutes. The conversation always follows the same pattern: during the second drink, a friend who knows the story mentions it to someone who doesn't. The newcomer's ears pick up, and he or she asks me about it. I give a two-minute synopsis and the reaction is always the same.

"Gee, you must be very brave to have gone through that."

I laugh and order another drink. "I don't remember ever feeling brave."

The next comment depends upon whether the listener is for or against gun control. "Surely," the listener says, "after this experience, you must be for (or against) it."

I don't have an answer in support of either side. The Frys were slaughtered with a shotgun our constitution says Smrekar had a right to own. Jay Fry died while reaching for his own firearm.

Yet a strong gun control law would not have saved anyone, either. Michael Drabing did not use a gun on the Schneider family, but they're dead just the same. If Smrekar did not have legal access to a shotgun, he would have been creative and acquired one.

I tell my listeners they'll have to look elsewhere for evidence to support their point of view. My stories from a small, peaceful town in the heart of Illinois can't help.

My listeners' next conclusion is that certainly I must now be in favor of capital punishment. Yet I can't help there, either.

The death penalty would not have deterred Smrekar because he never thought he was going to be caught. Nobody, especially him, commits a crime thinking he'll have to pay for it.

Justice would not be served by killing him. If the execution could bring back life, then yes, it would be worth it; certainly trading a Russell Smrekar for a Ruth Martin or a Mike Mansfield would be a bargain.

Many people said they wanted Smrekar executed. What they meant was, they wanted him to suffer the right amount, whatever that is, and the electric chair seemed like an obvious solution.

Yet Smrekar rotted in prison for about thirty-five years and then died . . . alone. Sounds fair to me.

Occasionally a liberal will comment that Smrekar must have had a terrible childhood to grow up with such a demented view of the world. I don't care if he had a terrible childhood; I just wanted him to have a terrible adulthood.

If we can't bring back life, or save life, or mete out justice, what's left? Only our memories of the past and how we feel about ourselves now remain. And these are the most important considerations of all: we are better than the Russell Smrekars of the world, aren't we? Or do we calmly look someone in the eye as a hood is drawn over his face and then, without emotion, pull a trigger or flip a switch and watch life slip away, like a spider washed down a drainpipe. Do we then joyride down the highway looking for campsites?

Russell Smrekar was not fit to live in this society. But we're not fit to kill him.

When my listeners realize I'm not going support to their pet theories, they wander off in search of another drink. Occasionally someone will stay and ask more fundamental questions: What made Smrekar tick? *Why* did he do those things? *How* could he do those things.

I don't know the answers. If pressed, I say he had a sociopathic personality. Was he driven by pure evil? Certainly his calm, cold demeanor and cold eyes when I confronted him in his dorm room scared me in a way I've never felt before or since.

Maybe he wasn't driven by evil; he seemed too passive for that. It didn't seem like a malevolent force, as much as the absence of any force at all, including feeling that he shouldn't do something because, well, it just wasn't right.

On the other hand, must evil be forceful? Maybe evil is simply a complete lack of conscience.

I've met others, similar in type to Smrekar, whose only difference appeared to be that they were afraid they'd get caught. Smrekar never thought he'd get caught and acted accordingly.

I don't know how Smrekar got that way. I wouldn't know how to change him. Is there a rehab program for people like him? I can't imagine, in my wildest dreams, that there is such a program.

That usually finishes anyone still listening. Once, though, someone stayed through my non-evidence and my non-theories and my non-solutions and asked what the experience had done to me.

The question caught me by surprise. I sipped my drink and said something about guilt about Mike Mansfield, that I thought about it every day, that it gave me a new perspective with which to judge the ups and downs of my life, that it made me feel much, much older.

I tried to finish answering the question, but damn, I really don't know the answer to that one either.

Chapter XXIII

Years have passed. Smrekar died after confessing to the four murders. Life has gone on. For some of us, though, questions remain that may never be answered.

Why was Smrekar in Lincoln three days after he was expelled and, we assume, apparently had driven home to Joliet, a hundred miles from Lincoln? Where was he going to cook the meat he had stolen?

He was not hiding in a dorm. The dorms are too small for him to live there unnoticed, and the students were furious at him, assuming he had stolen so many stereos and whatever from them during his freshman year. So where was he those days?

If he was guilty of burglarizing the dorm room, why did he agree to a lie detector test?

Five minutes after he was expelled from Lincoln College, he told me he was going to drop out of school the next day. What kind of mind thinks like that?

When he realized he had a terminal illness, he admitted to killing Ruth Martin and Mike Mansfield. When asked why he didn't admit to the murders earlier, he said he thought he'd get a pardon for the two murders for which he was convicted.

Smrekar was found guilty of first-degree murder for killing a man and his pregnant wife at point blank range with a shotgun. He thought he would get a pardon?

Smrekar apparently came to Lincoln from . . . Joliet? He went to Ruth Martin's house, waited until she was alone in her home, broke into the house and killed her, put the body in the trunk, drove to the interstate construction site, and buried her. Then he drove her car to Bloomington and abandoned it in the parking lot of the local Holiday Inn and . . . went home? How did he do that? Alone?

I never heard from Mike Mansfield's family. Perhaps the detective thought my letter would cause more pain and he decided not to forward it. Or maybe they just didn't want to talk about it anymore.

The afternoon of New Year's Eve, Mike Mansfield received a phone call, then told his family that he'd be gone about an hour. He left his home without taking a car and was never seen again. Who called him? Who picked him up?

Surely not Smrekar. Mike was a smart student; he would not agree to take a ride with the man he was soon to testify against. So who called him and picked him up?

When Russ admitted to killing Ruth Martin and Mike Mansfield, he gave an approximate location of where he buried Ruth, but never said anything about the location of Mike's grave. He tried to help the police recover Ruth Martin's body, but, to my understanding, said not a word about the location of Mike Mansfield. Why not? Would the location of the grave have implicated an accomplice?

Where is Mike Mansfield's body?

Who was the man in the restaurant who begged me to stop talking about the murders decades after they happened?

What happened to Patty Davis? I have searched the internet for years and have come across no sign of her.

It's possible she has died, or eventually married someone else and lived with her married name.

Five years ago, I reconnected with a high school class-mate who was a retired homicide detective for the Chica-go Police Department. I told him about the case and some of these questions. He shook his head and said, "Mike, even in a lot of the open-and-shut cases, there are ques-tions that are never answered."

• • •

To the victims and their still-grieving families; to Barba-ra; to Bill and Tom, the Lincoln detectives who worked so hard on the cases; to detective Phil Barille of the Roll-ing Meadows Police Department who kept the case alive for decades; to all of our supportive friends and relatives; to the wonderful, charming, goofy students; to the facul-ty—also wonderful, charming and goofy:

Charles Dickens had Tiny Tim finish *A Christmas Carol* with this: "God Bless us everyone."

I'd like to finish my story with the same sentiment.

Well, maybe not Russ Smrekar.

• • •

There are so many lingering memories from the year Smrekar was sent to prison.

It was graduation day—a warm, sunny day in May as the students, parents, and faculty crowded into the old gymnasium to finish the year and say goodbye. I saw the mother of Mitch Bernstein sitting next to an empty chair, so I sat down next to her. She and I knew each other fairly well by then, and I wanted to share this moment of triumph with her. What a triumph it was.

Mitch was one of those success stories newspapers often share at graduation time. He had cerebral palsy. Mitch had fought and scratched his way through two years on a campus that really wasn't equipped for him. When he talked, he was hard to understand at first, and it was painful to watch him walk. He wasn't brilliant, and his illness had left him a little shy about people and stubborn about everything else.

His constant smile never told how difficult life really was for him. His mother worried, of course, because she *knew*, but he never let on to the rest of us.

Al Pickering had made him assistant manager of the basketball team. Mitch couldn't do much more than hold out the towels to strong-legged athletes who were coming out of a game, but he was happy to do it, happy to be a part of it.

His shyness was caused by self-doubt—could people really like someone who looked and talked and walked like he did? We'd try to answer his doubts with wise-cracks because straightforward signs of affection would make him feel different, single him out once again. He loved it when we kidded him about being a lush, which he wasn't, or being horny, which he probably was.

A typical prayer meeting invitation would go like this:

"Mitch, you coming with us?"

"Oh, uh, I don't know."

"Don't give me that Mitch. I know you're lusting after a rum and coke, and the bartender will probably kick us out if old Boozer Bernstein isn't there to jack up the tab. What do you mean you don't know? Get in the damn car."

Mitch would get in the car with eyes bright and his smile restored. As we'd drive to the bar, we'd wonder if we could go through life misshapen like he was and not complain, give excuses, or turn bitter.

So that sunny morning, Mrs. Bernstein and I waited together for Mitch. The dean finally read Mitch's name, and we watched as he stumbled and lurched across the stage, grinning his great big grin and trying not to lose his graduation cap.

Immediately, the crowd jumped to its feet and began clapping. I stood up with the rest thinking someone should write about Mitch and his moment of glory. I turned to Mrs. Bernstein to tell her that, but she was not standing. She was still sitting in her chair, the only person in the gym sitting down. She was bent over, her hands covered her face, and when I saw her body shake softly, I realized she was weeping.

I don't know why the sight of a brave woman crying at the wonder and triumph of her remarkable son triggered my memory, but it did. I stood there in the ramshackle Lincoln College gymnasium, amid the clapping and the shouts of "Way to go, Mitch!" and watched Mitch wave his diploma to the crowd with an even bigger smile, and I thought about another mother, Mrs. Mansfield, who perhaps because of me, would never see her son Mike graduate, and I cried, too.

● ● ●

The author, Mike Hartnett, and his wife Barbara near the beginning of their time as employees at Lincoln College.

The author, Mike Hartnett, and his wife Barbara near the end of their time as employees at Lincoln College.

Timeline of Events

- 1972 - Mike and Barbara Harnett move to Lincoln, Illinois. Both had jobs at Lincoln College.

- 1974-75 - The incidence of burglaries of dorm rooms at Lincoln College is up.

- September 1975 - Students catch Mike Mansfield trying to dump stolen record albums down the trash chute at a dorm. Mansfield and Russell Smrekar are eventually brought before the college's Judicial Board. Smrekar is expelled from the school.

- October 1, 1975 - Smrekar is arrested for stealing steak from the local Kroger grocery store.

- December 9, 1975 - The petty theft trial against Smrekar ends in a mistrial.

- December 31, 1975 - Mansfield is last seen by his parents in Rolling Meadows, Illinois.

- January 1976 - Smerker was to go on trial for the theft of the albums and a guitar. Key witness, Mansfield, does not appear.

- June 2, 1976 - Ruth Martin, who is supposed to be witness in the second petty theft trial for Smrekar, goes missing.

- August 1976 - Michael Drabing murders the Schneider Family.

- October 9, 1976 - Jay and Robin Fry are killed in their home.

- October 18, 1976 - Smrekar is arrested for the murders of the Frys upon arriving for this third petty theft trial date.

- February 1977 - Smrekar is on trial for the murders of Jay and Robin Fry. He is sentenced to 300 years with eligibility for parole in nine years.

- February 1978 - A grave near McLean, Illinois, is dug up in search for the body of Ruth Martin. No remains are found.

- January 31, 1979 - The Appellate Court upholds Smrekar's sentencing.

- October 28, 2011 - Smrekar dies in prison at the age of 56 after having confessed to killing both Ruth Martin and Mike Mansfield. He provides clues to her whereabouts, but no body is recovered.

- January 2017 - Police search a Will County Illinois residence, presumably for the remains of Mike Mansfield. None are found.

About the Author

Mike Hartnett is a retired high school English/Speech teacher and business journalist (magazine columnist and editor and newsletter publisher), winning awards from the American Society of Business Press Editors. He led a memoir-writing group for the Douglas County Senior Citizen Center and is currently a co-leader of a men's writing group at the Douglas County Jail.

Mike is the co-author of a play, *Worthy of the Name*, which was presented at Chicago's Cultural Affairs Center, and a collaborator of a readers' theater production, *Prose & Cons, Voices From Behind Bars*.

Photo by Michelle Kelly

WWW.MEADOWLARK-BOOKS.COM

Specializing in Books by Authors from the Heartland since 2014

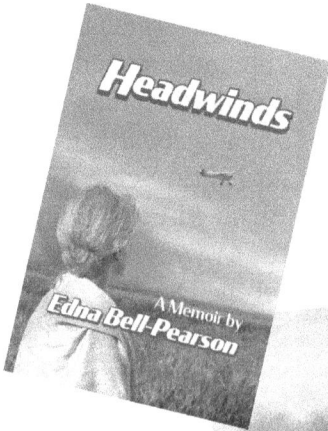

Headwinds

A Memoir by
Edna Bell-Pearson

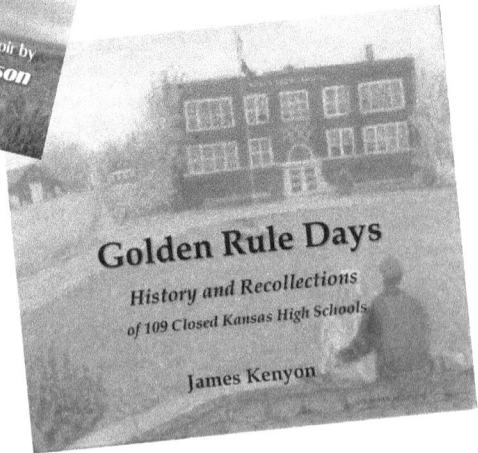

Golden Rule Days

History and Recollections
of 109 Closed Kansas High Schools

James Kenyon

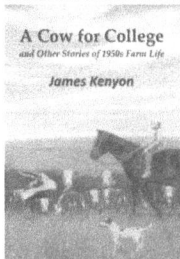

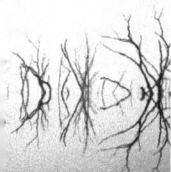

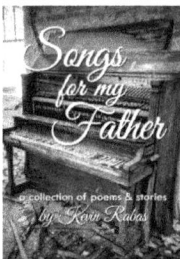

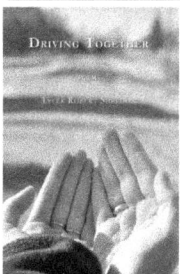

Books are a way to explore, connect, and discover. Reading gives us the gift of living lives and gaining experiences beyond our own. Publishing books is our way of saying—

We love these words,
we want to play a role in preserving them,
and we want to help share them with the world.

Meadowlark Press
— since 2014 —

meadowlarkbookstore.com